D1297650

1969

966.9   371575
  H
Hilton
Highly irregular.

Little Rock Public Library

HIGHLY IRREGULAR

ALSO BY BRUCE HILTON

The Delta Ministry
My Brother Is a Stranger

HIGHLY
IRREGULAR

by BRUCE HILTON

THE MACMILLAN COMPANY

COLLIER-MACMILLAN LTD., LONDON

THIS BOOK IS DEDICATED TO

John, Mike, Ray, Tony, Nick and John,

WHO DARED TO DREAM,

AND TO

Dave and Laveta Hilton,

FOR THE YEARS THEY GAVE NIGERIA

Copyright © 1969 by Bruce Hilton

All rights reserved. No part of this book may be reproduced or transmitted in any form or by any means, electronic or mechanical, including photocopying, recording or by any information storage and retrieval system, without permission in writing from the Publisher.

Library of Congress Catalog Card No. 70-93720

First Printing

The Macmillan Company
Collier-Macmillan Canada Ltd.,
Toronto, Ontario

Printed in the United States of America

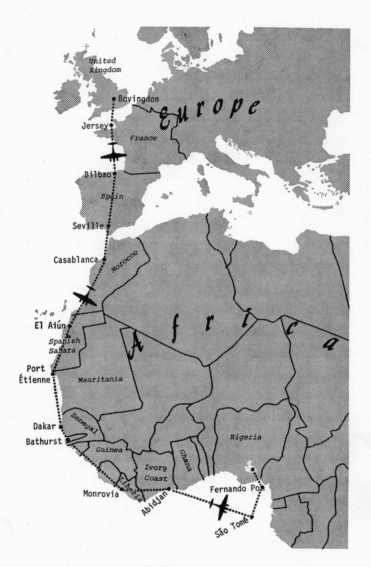

Voyage of the Faithful Annie

371575

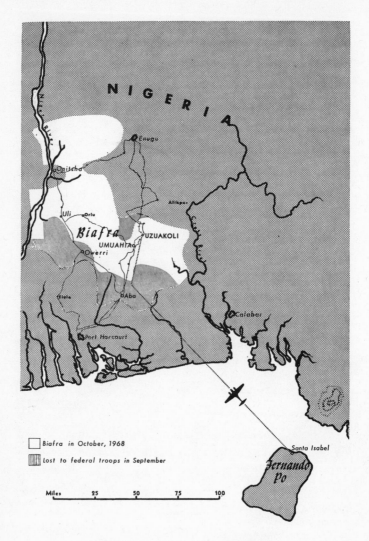

The Last Flight of Mike-Golf

Guillaumet was one among those bold and generous men who had taken upon themselves the task of spreading their foliage over bold and generous horizons. To be a man is, precisely, to be responsible. It is to feel shame at the sight of what seems to be unmerited misery. . . .

There is a tendency to class such men with toreadors and gamblers. People extol their contempt for death. But I would not give a fig for anybody's contempt for death. If its roots are not sunk deep in an acceptance of responsibility, this contempt for death is the sign either of an impoverished soul or of youthful extravagance.

— *Wind, Sand and Stars*

August 5, 1968

COUNTING the families, the crew, and members of the press, there must have been twenty-five or thirty people milling around the two planes.

It wasn't the kind of sight to which Bovingdon Air Force Base was accustomed, with women and children examining the airplanes, talking, shaking hands or kissing good-bye.

Nicholas Taaffe, pilot of one of the planes, waved his big hands enthusiastically as he answered questions from a BBC-TV interviewer. He was a bear of a man, just twenty-four, with an American-style crew cut and a ready grin. He looked eighteen.

John Smith, pilot of the other plane, was back in the hangar. He didn't especially like journalists. When he came out to say a word to Nick you could see that, despite his straight, almost military bearing, the top of his unruly shock of brown hair reached only to Nick's nose.

He flashed a quick smile at Sue, standing nearby holding their two-year-old daughter, Sennen-Dee, and then ducked into the plane.

The two planes squatted side by side in the midst of the crowd, gleaming in new paint and wax. The yawning cavern of Hangar Two, its doors open, made them look even smaller than they were. Faintly through the white paint you could see the RAF roundel, target-like, which had been the planes' identification until just a month ago.

A pair of RAF instructors, who a month before had used these planes or others like them to teach student pilots the rudiments of twin-engine flight, wandered into the circle and stopped a minute to examine the tailplane of one of the aircraft.

Young Michael Draper—thin and wiry like John, but at twenty-four fifteen years his junior—came trotting back from the RAF weather office with a sheaf of air charts in one hand. The weather was clearing all over southern England, he told John. But there would be heavy clouds, fog and rain at Guernsey, their first stop.

He showed the chart to Carol, his fiancée, an auburn-haired beauty in a miniskirt, and to Sue.

Anthony Stancomb was watching the scene through the viewfinder of a 16-mm movie camera. He moved in close to a group of people talking, and then flopped down on his stomach for a silhouette shot of the airplane wing. A tall, lean twenty-four-year-old whose speech and bearing spoke of good family and the best private schools, Tony merely grinned when somebody in the crowd joked about his marriage to his camera.

Ray Roberts was checking the boxes of medical supplies and the spares in the planes, making sure they wouldn't slide around in flight. In his late thirties, solidly built, Ray wore glasses and close-cropped black hair. When he was finished inside the plane, he fished his Rolleiflex out of a duffle bag and joined Tony in making shots of the crew, the families and the planes. His wife, Maxine, laughed and talked with Barbara Taaffe, Nick's bride of two months.

Nick's copilot, John Desborough, knelt under the wing and squinted up into the wheel well for the third time. He was a flier with the National Air Guard and, like John, liked to check everything at least twice before starting engines.

It was time to go. The six crew members were edging toward their planes, still talking, but glancing more and more frequently toward one another and toward their aircraft. There were no tears from the ladies; everybody was laughing, smiling and waving as though this were the start of a fortnight's holiday in Spain.

John Smith, Mike and Ray climbed into the gray and white plane; Nick, Tony and John Desborough disappeared into its all-white twin.

A reporter from *The Times* of London walked around the wing of John's plane, past the port engine and the big wooden propeller. He thumped the side of the fuselage, and was surprised to discover that it was tightly stretched canvas over a thin framework. He peered in a cabin window—the plane was small enough that he could look straight in without raising up on his toes—at the luggage and boxes of spare parts piled inside.

He moved away as the props began to turn over, and turned away from the rush of wind as the engines began to roar. He watched the planes waddle down the taxiway, first John's and then Nick's, to the end of the runway. Then with a roar they took off, one at a time, down the runway, lifting quickly and making a left turn to disappear toward the south.

"I wouldn't fly as far as Basingstoke in one of those things," the reporter said. "Much less across the Sahara Desert to Biafra."

2

When the wild ducks or the wild geese migrate in their season, a strange tide rises in the territories over which they sweep. As if magnetized by the great triangular flight, the barnyard fowl leap a foot or two into the air and try to fly. . . .

The call that stirred you must torment all men. Whether we dub it sacrifice, or poetry, or adventure, it is always the same voice that calls. But domestic security has succeeded in crushing out that part in us that is capable of heeding the call. We scarcely quiver; we beat our wings once or twice and fall back into our barnyard.

—*Wind, Sand and Stars*

THE WHOLE thing had been Nick Taaffe's idea.

Sitting around the Bovington aerodrome restaurant in June, he had been reading the London papers, which had suddenly blossomed with stories about Biafra.

During the preceding fall, there had been no British journalists covering the Biafran side of the civil war, but now it seemed the papers were full of pictures of the hungry children. Six thousand a day were dying of starvation, the *Sketch* said.

Nick had read that 13 million people, more than half of them Ibo tribesmen, were fighting for independence from Nigeria, and now were besieged in an area no bigger than the state of Vermont.

Attempts to get food through the blockade were not working. The Red Cross had been forced to stop its food flights from the Spanish island of Fernando Po, and the risky night flights made by church-supported groups from another island were continually harassed.

More than a million people inside Biafra were refugees, wandering homeless from village to village in search of food. The harvest was gone, and people were eating the seed yams they should be planting for the next crop.

To Nick the answer seemed simple enough. He was known around the airfields as a guy who always said exactly what he thought and who tore with tremendous energy into any project that captured his enthusiasm. Now, he reasoned, it was time for him to go to Biafra. There were not enough planes and pilots taking food to the hungry children. Obviously, people who knew how to fly planes ought to go down there and help.

And Nick knew how to fly a plane. Flying, in fact, was what he liked to do best, and what he would prefer to do all the time. He had been trained both in the United Kingdom and in the United States; from the latter he had brought back a vocabulary of strange American flying terms like "gear" for undercarriage, "manifold pressure" for boost, and "eyeballing" for visual flight.

Even his wedding in May had involved flying. To the consternation of the vicar and of the bride's parents, he had arranged to have one of his pilot friends land a helicopter in the churchyard after the ceremony and carry the couple away.

Nick had been signed on by British Eagle Airlines

as a copilot, just in time to see the company go bank-
rupt. The severance pay was good, and Nick with his
extra energy always found something to keep him busy.
But he wasn't spending as much time in the air as he
wanted.

While he was mulling over the Biafra stories, Nick
called John Smith, whom he had met at the Blackbushe aerodrome, southeast of London. John, a commercial pilot with more than a thousand hours' experience, had seen the stories about starving children
too, and was, he said, "hopping mad." He had been
wondering if there were not some way to help. Besides,
he said, he had been looking for a job that would take
him and his family to foreign shores, where he could
make a living at flying. Maybe there was a possibility
in connection with aid to Biafra.

Soon they had agreed to try together to find the
necessary support to go to Biafra. It was an unspoken
agreement from the first that they would try to get two
planes, since each man thought of himself as a *pilot*,
not as a copilot.

They set out eagerly to collar friends, relatives and
acquaintances—anyone who might contribute to the
cause. But the fund grew very slowly. The few
individuals they knew who had real money seemed
more interested in helping through what they called
regular channels. They contributed to the Red Cross,
or to Christian Aid or Oxfam, a pair of British-based
world relief agencies.

John tried to point out that the Red Cross had
stopped flying to Biafra, and that most of the involvement of the other two so far had been in supporting
the Red Cross effort.

But the money did not come in.

Friends in the National Air Guard, a semiofficial
flying organization supported by the government, were

interested in helping. But a look at the Guard's constitution revealed that this kind of involvement—especially in a country not even recognized by the British government—was impossible.

After nearly a month of looking, the pair heard from a friend, an Englishwoman whose husband was Biafran, about a Save Biafra Committee.

"Give them a try," she said. "You've tried everybody else."

So one afternoon in July they sought out the committee's tiny office, on the third floor over a garage and a printing plant. The area was so obscure the taxi driver had to look up the location of the street, and when they arrived it was obvious that the neighborhood was in an advanced stage of decay.

The office, when they climbed up to it, was the kind of place that would have been instantly recognizable to anyone who had been involved in the peace or civil-rights movements anywhere. The wall was papered with posters, attacking everything from British guns in Nigeria to American arms in Vietnam and apartheid in Johannesburg. A mimeograph machine, with paper, ink and rags filled a table along one wall. Piles of leaflets, fact sheets, warnings and announcements filled another table on the opposite wall.

There were a couple of filing cabinets, an electric heater in the middle of a bare floor, and a desk piled high with letters and more mimeographed materials next to the window.

The man at the desk, in a rumpled gray business suit, was Peter Cadogan—a man who was once described as Britain's only full-time, professional agitator.

Mr. Cadogan (pronounced "ka-DUG-an") looks more like a middle-aged bank clerk than the man who organized the protest against the visit of Greek royalty, the march on the American bomber bases in Britain, and dozens of other campaigns against war and injustice.

Officially he is national secretary for the Committee of One Hundred, an antiwar group that grew out of the old ban-the-bomb and anti-nuclear-testing movements. The committee, like Cadogan, is committed to nonviolent protest. During the last few years it had fought for causes generally considered wildly radical and had eventually seen many of them become accepted by the general public.

Cadogan was seeing Nick and John, however, in one of his other capacities: as unpaid secretary-organizer of the Save Biafra Committee. Organized just one month before, the committee spent much of its time lobbying and letter-writing to get the Wilson government to stop supplying heavy arms to Nigeria. Members were now organizing a support-Biafra rally to be held in Trafalgar Square in another week.

John and Nick were not too comfortable in this colorful, messy office, and they were a little uneasy with Peter Cadogan. The place reeked of politics, and neither of the pilots wanted anything to do with politics. The feeding of hungry children, they felt, should be nonpartisan. They had already agreed that they would fly food not only into Biafra, but into the war-torn parts of Federal Nigeria as well.

But they were running out of potential backers, and if this man could get them money, they were willing to use him and his committee to get the job done.

Cadogan was uneasy too. Save Biafra Committee was not in the relief business. Its purpose was to push for the long-term solution to Biafra's hunger: an end to the war. He had no authority to offer the men help.

But their arrival coincided with a major concern of the committee. There were 3,000 tons of food from all over the world piling up in warehouses on the island of Fernando Po. The Red Cross seemed to be making only half-hearted attempts to fly it in, giving Nigerian antiaircraft fire as the reason.

Cadogan believed the real reason was political. He told John and Nick that the International Committee of the Red Cross was walking a political tightrope. It was afraid that further help to the Biafrans, a rebel people apparently doomed to failure, might permanently alienate the ICRC from the Federal Nigerians whose cooperation they must have in order to help all refugees after the war. It appeared that the war would be over by September.

Some Red Cross officials, Cadogan felt, went further than that—and had accepted the "quick-kill theory."

This argument, quite prevalent in the USA and in Great Britain that summer, held that the most merciful thing to do for the starving children of Biafra was to get the war over fast. Since shipping food to Biafra was bolstering the rebels' morale, it was prolonging the war—and, thus, the misery.

The best thing to do for Biafra, then, was to stop all aid and encouragement to its people, in hopes that its government would quickly surrender.

This line of thought was an especially popular one, of course, among those who favored Nigeria in the civil war. Many visitors to Lagos were coming back convinced of the soundness of this "mercy-killing" theory.

Cadogan, a rather sensitive and warm-hearted man, disagreed thoroughly and was incensed that anyone could adopt such a callous attitude toward individual human life, no matter how logical the argument.

Cadogan talked awhile with John and Nick, hearing their plans. Then, without consulting any of the other members of the committee, he made a decision.

If the airlift was really being held up for political reasons, then getting it moving again was legitimately part of his committee's business. He was willing to use these two pilots, who wanted so badly to get to Biafra, toward that end.

"Okay," he said. "We'll do what we can."

Cadogan had had years of experience in presenting unpopular ideas to the press, and in the next few weeks he used everything he had learned. First he went with Nick and John to the big national newspapers based in London. Papers such as the *Telegraph* and the *Times* often are willing to sponsor an expedition or a relief mission—especially one that combines a humanitarian or scientific goal with lots of headline potential.

But the papers were not interested in this project, which by now the pilots were calling Mercy Missions. The *Sketch* had already chartered one cargo plane full of food flown to Fernando Po; it was looking for something new in stunts. The *Sun* was in financial trouble, and the *News of the World* just was not interested. Neither were the *Times* or the *Telegraph*.

The last hope was the general public. On Friday, July 12, Peter Cadogan called a press conference at The Feathers, a popular pub just off Fleet Street. There was a good turnout; the reporters heard Nick and John describe their plan and heard Peter issue a plea to the public for funds.

The plan, as the reporters heard it, had come a long way from that first hazy notion in Nick's head. Nick talked about the Viking, a postwar RAF transport, which looks quite a bit like the faithful old DC-3 but is a good 100 miles an hour faster. Vickers had not built any new ones since 1949, and most of the models still flying were with outfits such as the Arab Legion and the Argentine Air Force. But since they were being replaced by bigger and faster planes, Nick knew where two of them could be bought cheaply.

John displayed a map of the territory they would have to cover en route to Fernando Po, the island in the Bight of Biafra from which the two planes would shuttle in food. Each plane could make two trips a day, carrying about two tons of food each time. They could do some things that were not practical for the big Constellations and DC-7s used by the airlift, he said. For example, the smaller planes could fly in the day-time because they could just skim the treetops, fooling the Nigerian radar and surprising the antiaircraft crews. And they could land on unpaved strips or even in cattle yards, bringing the food closer to where it was needed.

One of the big relief agencies, John explained, had indicated it might support the Mercy Missions shuttle, once the crews had arrived on Fernando Po and established their competence.

The reporters were intrigued by the story, and most of the papers the next day had stories about Mercy Missions. That was on a Saturday.

On the following Monday morning the mailman delivered more than 400 letters to the little third-floor committee office. They were from people who had seen the newspaper stories, and they contained more than $10,000 in cash and checks.

Three little girls in Bolton, in Lancashire, had spent all day Saturday going door-to-door, exchanging roses from their gardens for contributions to Mercy Missions. They sent $51.

One lady cashed an insurance policy and sent a check for $2,400.

A London girl sent $40 she had collected from friends, with a note: "I hope that you will be able to get to Biafra before too late."

The congregation of Westminster Synagogue sent a large donation.

Most of the checks were small—$10 to $20. Most were accompanied by notes: a typical one said, "This is a wonderful thing you are doing; God bless you."

During the week, the mails brought another $4,800.

An American living in Iceland had seen the story in the airmail edition of the London *Times*; he sent a check for $72. Alan Bridge and Ivor MacKany wrote: "Dear Sir, my friend Ivor and I have had a street stall. We are sending you the 12 shillings 5 pence [about $1.75] we made to help the Biafran children."

And a high official of the Moscow-Narodny Bank Ltd., a Russian financial institution, made a personal donation of $48.

It was a totally unexpected response.

Cadogan, like most people who must raise funds for "good causes," was aware that for ten years the interest of potential donors to such causes had been waning. Some experts blamed it on compassion fatigue—a numbing of the ability to feel and respond to human need because of the constant exposure to such need via TV and radio. Some said it was the continual portrayal of death and misery on TV, as in the Vietnam war reports.

Others blamed the impersonal face that the relief activities must show the giver because of their size. It isn't your neighbor or a man fallen by the wayside whom you help nowadays; it is some anonymous person thousands of miles away. The most efficient and effective way to bring him emergency relief is through an organization with the necessary expertise and long-term support—but there is not much satisfaction for the giver in that.

But Biafra somehow was getting through to people.

(The same thing was happening in the United States. Church World Service distributed some broadcast recordings of an interview with Dr. Ibiam, an Ibo leader who was president of the World Council of Churches. Not long afterward, Father Raymond Kennedy, an Irish priest who had spent his adult life in Biafra, introduced Biafran officials to a Hollywood press agent, Robert S. Goldstein. The CWS interviews and Goldstein's energetic PR work helped produce the greatest outpouring of relief funds from the American public since the end of World War II. More than a million dollars came to Church World Service alone in that first rush; Catholic Relief Services, the American Jewish Committee and other similar groups had the same kind of response.

(The idea that children were starving surely had much to do with the strong response. So did the "underdog" nature of Biafra's fight. But the Rev. John Abbott, director of information for Church World Service, points to a third factor. The Biafra story began to be told widely, he says, "just at the time when a newly relevant youth generation had lost its battle for McCarthy. Some of them turned to working for other candidates, but many of them said, 'Let's do something about Biafra.' "

(Certainly young people were a major factor in fund-raising, both in the USA and in Great Britain. College and high school youth all over the United States held car washes, bazaars, and dances. A church youth group in suburban Leonia, New Jersey—a town of 8,500 people—went from door to door on one Saturday and raised $2,700 for an ambulance for a refugee camp.)

In Great Britain, Mercy Missions caught the crest of this wave. And suddenly, after weeks of discouragement, it was in business. The pressure was now on to get going.

The planes had to be bought, checked, and made ready. Crews had to be recruited. Passports, visas, and landing permissions had to be secured from at least eight different countries in three different languages. And arrangements had to be made with the Biafrans to let the planes come in.

Nick's musings over the newspaper had suddenly produced a mountain of work, and there would be times when he wished he had stayed with the sports pages.

Pilots are widely dispersed over the face of the world. They land alone at scattered and remote airports, isolated from each other rather in the manner of sentinels between whom no words can be spoken. It needs the accident of journeyings to bring together here or there the dispersed members of this great professional family.

—*Wind, Sand and Stars*

WHILE Nick and John were out looking at airplanes and Peter Cadogan was making arrangements to fly to Biafra, as their advance man, Hannah Baneth was manning the office phone and typewriter—handling the details.

Hannah had walked in off the street one day, attracted by a letter from the Save Biafra Committee, which had been printed in the *Evening Standard*. She was a Jew, she said, a citizen of Israel although she had lived and worked in England for twenty years. As a child in Hamburg she had suffered all the indignities of being a Jew under Hitler, until her family finally fled to Israel.

She had heard the Ibo tribesmen, with their passion for education and their skill at trading, described as the Jews of Nigeria. And she had read of what seemed to be a campaign of genocide against the Ibos. She wanted to help stop it.

Hannah was a skilled typist and stenographer. She soon had the SBC files in order and had helped catch up on a pile of old correspondence.

Bright and friendly, with just a trace of German accent, she spent nearly every evening at the SBC office. And if her passion for detail sometimes irritated the more casual Cadogan—"Peter says I'm a bureaucrat"—even he admitted at times that she was nearly indispensable.

Now, for Mercy Missions, Hannah was performing the same unglamorous jobs. She acknowledged each of the 400 or more contributions, filed their addresses for future reference and sent each donor newsletters reporting on progress.

She helped arrange with the Bank of England and Lloyd's Bank for money to be available to the crew along the way and in Fernando Po—no easy trick, under England's strict exchange laws. Gasoline credit cards had to be procured—a much easier task thanks to the Esso people, who issued a card for each plane on the strength of a telephone call.

Liability insurance had to be bought for the planes, although its value may have been diminished (in this instance more than most) by the clause that excluded damage caused by "war risks, riots, strikes, civil commotion and malicious damage."

Meanwhile, Nick and John were discovering that the Vikings were too expensive for the Mercy Missions' budget. The cost of fuel for those big 1700-horsepower Hercules engines would soon be more than the original price of the planes. And they learned that government regulations for aircraft of that size would require both John and Nick to take additional training, costing several hundred pounds.

Nick had seen an advertisement in a flying magazine for a much smaller twin-engine plane, the Avro Anson. The company doing the advertising had eight Ansons on hand, bought in June from the Royal Air Force after the RAF had stopped using them.

John and Nick made a date to meet with Alec Dowse, the owner, and hurried out to Bovingdon Air Force Base, thirty miles north of downtown London. They looked at a few planes, talked price a while, and then called Hannah to tell her they had found the aircraft they wanted to fly to Biafra.

The Avro Anson had been known to RAF pilots as "Faithful Annie" for more than thirty years. An RAF squadron first took delivery of the squat, low-winged plane in 1936. It was used as a reconnaissance bomber, and its two Cheetah radial engines gave it what was then a fairly respectable speed for a bomber: 158 miles an hour.

Inside, it was a booby trap. Its passenger cabin tapered from about six feet of headroom near the front down to five feet near the entry door at the rear, so that forgetful crew members were always straightening up suddenly and bashing their heads against the ceiling. And the main wing spar ran through the fuselage at the bottom of the door between the passenger cabin and the cockpit. Eighteen inches high and six inches wide, it produced barked shins and loud curses any time someone tried to get through the door in a hurry.

But in the air she was a sweetheart. The cockpit gave the pilot and first officer plenty of room, and visibility in all directions was excellent, simply because the walls and roof were mostly glass. And the RAF pilots soon learned that she did exactly what you wanted her to do.

She was what pilots call a "forgiving" airplane; you could make minor errors like leveling off a couple of feet too high for a landing, and the Anson would survive the resulting thump.

She would even forgive that most embarrassing of pilot goofs, the gear-up landing. The wheels do not fold entirely inside the fuselage, even when the landing gear is retracted. They protrude just enough to keep the bottom of the fuselage from scraping the concrete. The wooden propellers would be smashed, of course, but it is easier to replace a prop than a fuselage.

"It's a plane of character," John Smith said much later, after he got to know the Anson. "You have to know it, and its tricks. But you can identify with it, and you come to like it very much."

The plane's reputation for being a lady in the air and a witch on the ground was enhanced by the fact that it was so difficult to taxi. It has no controllable tail wheel for steering, and the engines are too close to the fuselage to be much help in turning on the ground. Many an RAF student pilot has complained that he could "get her up and down, but can't drive her back to the hangar."

Much as the pilots liked her, Faithful Annie was obsolete as soon as she began flying. The Germans were building faster fighters, and the RAF Bomber Command was demanding bigger carrying capacity.

A plane that chugged along at 158 miles an hour, with only one defensive machine gun, was easy prey for a Messerschmitt 109. And when the Anson got to its target, it could drop only four 500-pound bombs— compared to its newer and bigger brother, the Avro Lancaster, which could drop ten times that many.

So early in World War II the Anson was converted to a trainer. Navigators, gunners and pilots all could learn their craft in Ansons, crisscrossing the British Isles by the hundreds in those frantic days. Most of the RAF's bomber pilots (and most airline pilots in the Commonwealth today) made the transition from single-engine to multi-engine flight by learning to fly an Anson.

Other Ansons became communications aircraft—the euphemism employed by air forces around the world for the planes that provide personal transportation for colonels and generals and give them the chance to earn their required monthly minimum flying time. Communications aircraft also carry spare parts from one air base to another, reporters and brass hats on inspection trips and urgent messages too secret for radio or cables. They are the air forces' equivalent of a jeep and are thus indispensable.

In this role, the Anson survived the war, and Avro went on building more when the war was over. In a day when planes became obsolete and were replaced as fast as new ones came off the drawing board, Faithful Annie was almost unique; she was one of the few aircraft in production before World War II to continue in production after the war was over. In all, Avro built 11,020 Faithful Annies. The last one came off the production line on May 27, 1952.

By then, this model plane was being used by the Israeli, Canadian, Afghan and Southern Rhodesian air forces, among others. And even after Avro stopped building them, the RAF continued to use them for another sixteen years.

The last eighteen Ansons were officially mustered out on June 28, 1968, with ceremonies at Bovingdon AFB that included a band, marching formations and speeches. Then six of the planes, washed and polished, came low in a line over the aerodrome in one last flyby. Most of the officers watching had trained in Ansons; for them it was the RAF's last remaining link, not only with the crucial days of the Battle of Britain, but with their own days as student pilots as well. Few of the journalists present were able to resist remarking that an era was ending.

It was just three weeks later that Nick and John arrived at Bovingdon to see about putting the Ansons back to work.

While Hannah and Peter arranged for payment and transfer of title for the two aircraft, John and Nick began recruiting crew members.

The first to get a call was Mike Draper, who was working as a bank clerk and living with his parents in Camberley, twenty-five miles southwest of London.

"How would you like to navigate an airplane for me?" John asked.

"Sure," said Mike.

"It's an Anson I'm taking to Africa."

"Why not?" said Mike.

Mike's confidence came from his knowledge of John Smith, not of Africa. A slender, pleasant young redhead, Mike had been the typical "airport kid." He had hung around the Blackbushe aerodrome, a former RAF base just south of Camberley, ever since he was old enough to go there by himself. He had become one of a large group of hobbyists, sort of birdwatchers to the aviation world, who try to see and record every different model of every type of airplane flying. He had edited *Blackbushe Movements*, a mimeographed newsletter reporting every transient plane that landed at the field.

Like all airport kids, Mike had dreamed of becoming a pilot himself, and hitched free air rides whenever he could. So far he had managed to get only twenty hours' experience as a student pilot.

He met John Smith one day in 1964, after he had begun working and taking flying lessons. John backed his car over Mike's motor scooter. John made it up by offering to take Mike along as navigator on a charter flight. They hit it off well and soon were flying together often.

In those days John often was one of the pilots trying to make an extra five pounds by flying flowers up from Cornwall in the spring or by delivering an urgently needed part from a London factory to a branch plant in the hinterlands. Mike had been glad to go along for the experience, and John, operating on a limited profit margin, was glad to have a navigator he did not have to pay. In the process, Mike had become a good navigator, and the two had developed the kind of teamwork where few words were needed. Each trusted the other to do his job.

So when John's phone call came, the fourth week in July, 1968, Mike didn't hesitate.

"One would sort of forgive me if I'd said, 'No, I don't quite think so,'" Mike said much later. "But I had every bit of confidence in John's flying.

"And when I thought of the humdrum life I'd led up to then . . . well, it would be something to write home about."

As a former airport kid, Mike still instinctively snatched at any chance to "build up time." And if a man could help out starving children, while exercising a craft for which he was prepared and which he enjoyed thoroughly, who could ask more?

Mike was also interested in the possibility, suggested by John, that after the Biafran crisis was over in a few months, there would always be other emergencies around the world. Airplanes could be instruments of mercy there too. This might grow into a full-time career in which the pay might not be as much as a bank clerk's, but conditions could be a whole lot more interesting and satisfying.

After he said yes, Mike had had a few sleepless nights. He was giving up a job which had plenty of security and the promise of regular promotions over the next forty years, even if it didn't pay much right now. He wondered if he were making a mistake.

And there was a vision that kept him awake nights, drawn from the comic books about World War II. He could picture a line of gunboats along the Nigerian shore, throwing up a solid wall of bursting shells, any one of which could blow a little Anson to pieces.

The final agreement was that Mike would go along as first officer and navigator for John, but would go only as far as Fernando Po. He would then stay on the island as ground-support and liaison officer while John and Nick flew the missions into Biafra and Nigeria.

Mike's fiancée, Carol, thought the trip was a good idea. In fact, they agreed as they talked it over that it might be the ideal place to start their marriage—a tropical island, with palm trees, beach and blue ocean. When Mercy Missions was established and Mike was making a regular salary, Carol would join him on Fernando Po and they would be married.

Nick invited as his copilot John Desborough, a stocky, handsome man several years older than himself.

Desborough had been one of the National Air Guard pilots who tried to get the organization to sponsor Mercy Missions and who had been deeply disappointed when that plan fell through. He jumped at the chance to go along.

Ray Roberts, John Smith's radio man, recruited himself.

A reasonably successful free-lance photographer, Ray had been trying to get into Biafra. Some of his journalist friends had already been there, and editors assured him there would be a market for any pictures he might take there.

But he had had trouble getting the newspapers for which he usually worked—the *Times*, the *Daily Express*, and the IPC press syndicate—to give him a letter stating that he was acting on their behalf. This was probably because they didn't want the responsibility in case something happened to him inside Biafra, Ray realized, but it made it difficult for him to raise the cash necessary to go. Biafra House, the unofficial embassy in London, was asking £150 ($360) from every journalist who wanted a visa. And the round-trip air fare was more than $300. The newspapers were willing to furnish him with credit cards for sending cables, but not with cash. The trip looked impossible.

Then one evening he saw a story in the local paper about the Biafra planes of Nicholas Taaffe, who lived just a few miles away. He tracked Nick down the next day at the Bovingdon aerodrome, where work had already begun on the two Ansons.

When Nick and John learned that Ray was a former RAF radio operator, and that he had spent six years in the service as a noncommissioned officer before being grounded by bad eyes, they asked him to join the crew.

Ray, it turned out, had spent many hours in Ansons and knew the radio equipment well.

Approaching forty and beginning to show middle-aged spread, Ray seemed a little abrupt to people who didn't know him. He affected a rather cynical air, almost as though he felt being a journalist required this of him. Then, just when he seemed to be most pompous and condescending, he would turn around and needle himself for his attitude.

Ray was also the most vehement of the group in denying that he was going to Biafra out of any humanitarian motive. In fact, he sometimes brought it up when no one had asked. "I can't stand do-gooders," he would say. And yet it turned out that he was the one member of the crew who had spent any appreciable amount of time working on local charity drives.

"Politics is phony," he would announce in a rich, bass voice. "A waste of time." And yet it turned out he was an active member of the Socialist party, and had been elected a councilman in Felixstoke, a town of 30,000 people, when he lived there.

Ray turned out to be one of the most efficient crew members, one of the hardest workers in Mercy Missions. But he also turned out to be the hard-luck guy. If something went wrong, it happened to Ray—even when, six weeks later, it came to the worst luck of the whole trip.

Anthony Stancomb didn't care much for the nickname Tony, but he bore graciously the fact that that's just what everybody called him. An easy-going young man with a dry sense of humor, he had got together with Mercy Missions through a friend of a friend and brought with him two skills the crew thought they might be able to use. He spoke six languages, and he was a professional film maker.

He was just getting started in his profession, operating from a flat in fashionable Chelsea. He had spent the previous two years as a rural development officer with Volunteers in Service Overseas—the British counterpart of the Peace Corps.

He had been in Swaziland, a tiny British colony near the southern tip of Africa surrounded on three sides by South Africa and on the fourth by Mozambique. There he had helped farmers organize a union, and had persuaded the men of a village to donate their labor to build a concrete dam, with cement donated from England. The dam provided a reservoir for the village, to the delight of the women, who had been walking more than a mile to get water for drinking and cooking.

Before Swaziland, Tony had been a student at St. Andrews, an exclusive university in Scotland. And before that he had spent most of his time in Europe, attending private schools and traveling widely in the summers.

All this travel had not blunted his appetite for seeing new places, however. The idea of going to Biafra appealed to both the traveler and the cinematographer in him.

He thought his experience with "proteins and calories and all that" in distributing food in Swaziland would probably be helpful to Mercy Missions. And it was hoped that he could produce an effective color film about the project and its first twenty or so flights into Biafra, to be used in raising more funds in England.

As the crew got acquainted and began to work together, it was John Smith, not Nick, who emerged as its leader. Soft spoken and precise in his speech, John

was as cool and careful as Nick was warm and
enthusiastic. The methodical way he did things inspired
confidence. His flying skill impressed even the old RAF
noncom, Ray Roberts: Ray once dropped his journalistic detachment long enough to tell a friend, "I'd fly
into the jaws of hell with John."

But there was a sense of caution in John's relations
with others. He seemed a little less able than the others
to kid himself.

At thirty-nine, John was a man who had had dreams
and had seen most of them vanish. After two years as
a police trainee and two years in the Army as a youth,
he had spent twelve years in business. He had started
his own company to repair textile machinery, building
it up until he had thirty employees, and then had seen
it go down the drain in 1954 for lack of capital. He
had started again, selling printing machinery, and had
worked up through sales manager to being a director
of a group of small businesses involved in aviation. In
1963, that had failed. He had spent the last six years
in aviation, mostly as a flight instructor and charter
pilot. It had been a time of financial uncertainty, of
irregular hours, and of a continual need to hustle for
the extra trip, the extra shilling. And always, with every
new acquaintance, the hope that this might mean the
start of some new venture that would not only help put
him back on top but also would be worth doing for its
own sake.

At his age, John didn't have the luxury of laughing
at himself quite as much as Tony, Nick and Michael
could at twenty-four. There was a growing sense of the
race against time, the feeling that it might already be
too late.

Mercy Missions might be the last chance. It
appealed to his sense of outrage over the needless

deaths of the Biafran children. And it offered the possibility of beginning again outside the United Kingdom—of making the fresh start.

Sue agreed. As soon as the mission was under way, she was planning to sell the furniture and bring Sennen-Dee to join him on Fernando Po.

It took three full weeks, working eighteen hours a day, to get the two Ansons ready to go to Biafra. Officially, the work was to be carried out by Alec Dowse's organization as part of the sale price—about $4,800 for each plane. But the Mercy Missions crews could not stay away from Hangar Two at Bovingdon; they helped with much of the work.

The most important thing was qualifying each plane for its "C of A"—the Certificate of Airworthiness issued by the Board of Transport. The Ansons had been built to RAF specifications and operated under military regulations; now they would have to undergo dozens of small changes to engines, auxiliary systems and airframes to meet the stiffer safety requirements for planes in civilian use.

Besides what was required by law, there were changes necessary to turn the Ansons into efficient cargo carriers. This was mostly a matter of removing the seats, carpeting, toilet, navigation tables and anything else that obstructed the cargo space or was unnecessary weight.

Just behind the forward cabin bulkhead they installed two big oil drums, lying lengthwise, one on each side of the door into the pilots' cockpit. These were connected, by a complicated series of hoses and valves, to the engines' fuel system. When filled, they would increase the Anson's normal range of 400 miles to more than 650 miles.

The circular RAF symbols and the RAF registration numbers had to be painted out and replaced by a huge red cross and the newly assigned civilian registration numbers. Nick's plane had to be completely repainted a sparkling white, since its brown-and-green camouflage made it look too much like a war plane. John's plane already bore the traditional paint scheme for communications aircraft, white on top and gray on the bottom, with a blue trim line between.

It was the civilian registration, assigned by the Board of Transport, which gave the two Ansons the only names they would have through everything that followed: Mike-Golf and Mike-Hotel.

In Great Britain an aircraft's number is actually a list of letters painted on the side and the wing and used by the pilot to identify himself to control towers via radio. John's Anson was registered as G-AWMG, and Nick's was G-AWMH.

On the radio, the pilot was required to use a specific word for each identification letter, chosen by the International Civil Aviation Organization so it would not be misunderstood in any language, even if garbled by static. Thus John's G-AWMG would be known to control towers, on first contact, as Golf-Alfa-Whisky Mike-Golf. Acknowledging later transmissions, he would use only the last two letters, Mike-Golf.

And that's what they came to be called for the brief but rather eventful period that remained for the two Ansons. No sentimental nicknames, no tricky puns—just Mike-Golf and Mike-Hotel.

The third "Mike"—redheaded Michael Draper—first saw the planes on Saturday, July 27, when he drove out to Bovingdon at John's invitation. They were painting the big red crosses on Mike-Hotel, and several photographers were on hand to catch John, Nick and Mike posing in front of the gleaming white

Anson. One photographer insisted on putting Tess, John's black Labrador retriever, in the navigator's seat and getting a shot of her and John as cockpit partners.

Bill Adams and Alec Dowse were still scurrying about, bleary eyed from lack of sleep, making final adjustments. Everyone was hoping for takeoff on August 1, the following Thursday.

Alec showed Mike and John how the work was progressing and told them he had decided to hold back two of his remaining six Ansons, in case Mercy Missions wanted to buy them after getting under way.

The days and nights sped by. By day, the crew was either helping at the aerodrome or rushing around London buying khakis, picking up passports or arranging for visas.

By night they discussed routes and flight plans, spreading the big charts out on a kitchen table. It took ten big Operational Navigation Charts, each one five feet long and three and one-half feet wide, to cover the 4,000 miles.

The most direct route would have been straight south across France and Spain to Tangier, then right down across the Sahara to Abidjan, capital of Ivory Coast. But the airports were 500 miles apart—getting close to the limit of the Ansons' range. And for more than 1,500 miles the maps showed little more than camel trails, with the ominous legend DATA INCOMPLETE.

It was unanimously decided to go down around the hump of west Africa, following the thin line of towns on the coast, squeezed between the Atlantic and the ocean of sand.

The yardstick was brought out, and tentative course lines drawn between places with such exotic names as Seville, Casablanca, El Aiún, Dakar, and Abidjan.

Nick was fascinated by the idea of being "captain"

of his own plane. He often arrived at briefing meetings with a new badge, some insignia of rank, a pair of epaulets, or a set of pilot's wings patterned after the military uniform wings. He took a terrific ribbing from the rest of the crew but insisted on turning his new khakis into a fairly impressive uniform, complete with a billed captain's hat with gold decoration.

John was willing to wear the four stripes on his epaulets, signifying his rank as captain, but like the rest of the crew, he stowed most of the badges and insignia Nick brought him in his suitcase. If the time came, as Nick argued, when they really needed to impress somebody, they could always dig them out.

On Sunday the 28th, John Smith and Mike Draper studied the electrical and fuel systems under the tutelage of Alec Dowse and a couple of the RAF officers on the base. Monday was spent shopping, and John worked his way through a foot-long list of telephone calls. When they got back to Bovingdon, they found that both planes had had their engine tests. The compasses had been swung, and the planes were ready for test flights the next day.

Mike was up early on Tuesday, driving to the busy London airport for his second set of inoculations and looking for a spare set of air charts. Employees of British Overseas Airways Company, BOAC, who were usually preoccupied with planes ten times as big, went out of their way to help him on both counts.

A TV team with two camera crews from the news program *Twenty-Four Hours* was on hand when Mike returned to Bovingdon. Peter Cadogan had persuaded the news show to send its top correspondent, who was rather belligerently dubious about the whole project until John Smith spent half an hour taking him around.

The friendship was to pay off later, at a critical time.

That afternoon the weather, which had been perfect for days, began to turn sour. Low black clouds moved in, and a light continuous drizzle began.

There was time for John and Nick to make quick test flights, but if conditions got any worse they would not be able to take off for Guernsey and Seville the next day.

Mike-Golf's second test flights, to check the radios, was not an auspicious one.

Carol Libby, Mike's girl, had been invited to go along. It was her first ride in any kind of plane except an airliner. And Mike, though riding the copilot's seat, was making his first flight in a twin-engined plane. Tony was also aboard, camera in hand.

One of the airport crew laboriously turned the big wooden propellers a couple of revolutions by hand to loosen them up, and then John began grinding the starter.

He carefully tested each engine, at idling speed and at full power, and then swung Mike-Golf into position at the end of the runway for the final checks before takeoff: "Trim: neutral. Throttle friction: adjusted. Temps and pressures: within limits. Ignition switches: caged on. Pressure head heater: on." And so on, as Mike read off the list, John made the checks, and Tony peered out at the low-hanging gray clouds.

Then the engines began to roar, John released the brakes, and Mike-Golf surged down the shiny wet runway, picking up speed quickly, and then leaped up into the clouds.

John, his eyes fixed on the blind-flying instruments, was beaming broadly. Tony and Mike and Carol grinned at one another.

It was John who quit laughing first; then Mike,

because he had the only other pair of earphones. He heard John say, "Ah, Bovingdon tower, this is Mike-Golf."

"Go ahead, Mike-Golf."

"Ah, Bovingdon, do you know where we are?"

"No, Mike-Golf, but you can't be far."

"Bovingdon, I hate to say this, but we seem to be lost."

Even the next twenty minutes, during which the Bovingdon tower finally located Mike-Golf on radar and steered it back home, through the rain, failed to dampen the spirits of the crew aboard. Mercy Missions was, literally, off the ground at last.

Thursday dawned black and wet; flying was out of the question. Friday and Saturday were no better, and it didn't help to discover, from the RAF meteorologist, that both Guernsey and Seville, their scheduled first-day stops, were enjoying bright sunshine.

The crew kept busy with odd errands; John and Nick went to London to sign travelers' checks, and Mike rounded up one more life jacket. They discovered a company near the London airport called International Aeradio, which not only had the charts they needed for a complete set, but also gave them a complete spare set free.

Sunday was still murky, and the crew spent the day going over the charts once more and trying to reload the planes so the cargo would be closer to the center of gravity. But during the next morning the clouds swept away to the south. By noon, the weatherman said, it would be all right to take off. And the friends, family and press began gathering at Bovingdon to say goodbye.

4

What constitutes the dignity of a craft is that it creates a fellowship, that it binds men together and fashions for them a common language.

—*Wind, Sand and Stars*

J O H N Smith reached down to the ship-type compass just in front of his right knee and set the lubber line for 202 degrees.

The Anson was still climbing toward 3,000 feet; all the panel instruments were "in the green," reading just the way they should.

To the left, a mound of smog that reached several thousand feet above them indicated the presence of London; to the right, Mike could see the town of Windsor but not the castle.

The cockpit was like a greenhouse, with thirteen big panes of glass beside, before and above them. John was in the pilot's seat, on the left; Mike's seat was on the right and set back six inches. Ray rode a moveable jump seat in the doorway between the pilots' cockpit and the passenger cabin; he actually was sitting on the steel spar, six inches wide and eighteen inches high, which joined and supported the two wings.

Takeoff from Bovingdon had been at one o'clock, and by 1:30 they were crossing the narrow strip of water between the southern coast and the Isle of Wight, headed out over the Channel.

By then John had trimmed the ship for straight and level, and Mike had determined their ground speed

(112 miles an hour) by seeing how long it took to travel from one known point to another. Ray had tuned in the Guernsey radio beacon, so John could steer the plane directly to the island merely by always pointing the ship in such a way as to keep a pair of white needles centered on the dial in the middle of the windscreen, just above the instrument panel. Ray had tidied up the rear cabin and was now pointing his Rolleiflex out a side window at Nick's plane, off to the right and a little behind them.

It was a good feeling as England slipped out of sight behind them. For three weeks they had been working frantically to get the planes ready and to make all the arrangements for their stops in Africa; then when they were all ready to go they had suffered four miserable days of waiting for good weather. Now, officially out of the country, they could at last feel they were on their way.

The feeling did not go away even when the heavy gray clouds predicted by the weatherman began looming up, right on schedule and right on course. Soon they were in the soup, barely able to make out Nick's navigation light winking red on his left wingtip.

John went on instruments, keeping on course solely by reference to the dials clustered in front of his control wheel.

The rain began pelting the windscreen and drumming on the canvas roof. And it was not long after that that the crew discovered a major fault in the Avro Anson Mark 21 airplane: it leaked like a paper umbrella.

The water first began trickling in around the lower edge of the side windows. Then it began coming in the ceiling—either between the canvas and the glass on top, or right through the canvas. Soon John's khaki pants were sodden. Mike's chart for the Bovingdon–Guernsey run was soaked and limp, and the course lines he had drawn in ink were beginning to run. His red hair was soaking wet too.

Unfortunately, the bottom of the airplane didn't leak as much as the top. The water that came streaming in through the roof didn't leave nearly as fast, and soon the cockpit floor was covered with sloshing water. Ray began to look around for a can for bailing the plane out like a boat, not so much for comfort as for getting rid of the extra weight of all that water, which might overload the plane.

They went on like that for an hour. Guernsey aerodrome advised them that its ceiling was down around 200 feet. John told the controller he didn't have equipment modern enough to make an instrument approach for that low a ceiling, and he was advised to try either Bournemouth, back on the Channel coast, or the island of Jersey, a little farther on.

There was little sentiment for going back to England, after all the good-byes. And the radar base at Jersey came through loud and clear on the radio, reporting a 500-foot ceiling.

This was enough height, John felt, and they swung left toward Jersey, just twenty-five miles to the southeast. And fifteen minutes later, with the radar controller on the ground monitoring their course and glide path, they broke out of the clouds at 500 feet. The runway lights of the Jersey field were lined up exactly where they belonged, half a mile ahead. John's plane touched down with a satisfying "chirp" of the wheels, and a few minutes behind came Nick's.

There was a frightening moment when Nick's plane, near the end of its landing run, suddenly swerved off the paved runway and onto the grass. But the soggy ground slowed up the plane and stopped the groundloop.

The crews climbed out, glad to be there. It was still

British soil, but the island was in the Gulf of Saint-Malo, surrounded on three sides by France; it was the next best thing to actually being on foreign soil. It was obvious they could not go on to their destination for tonight, Seville, because of the weather, so they decided to make the best of it and enjoy the Isle of Jersey. Mike Draper, who had never been away from England except for one quick trip to Paris, was especially looking forward to it.

But before they left there, they were to get pretty sick of it and to wonder whether the trip wasn't somehow jinxed. Bound for Africa, 4,000 miles away, they were to spend the next four days in the rain on Jersey, 160 miles from home.

And now, having spoken of the men born of the pilot's craft, I shall say something about the tool with which they work—the aeroplane.

—*Wind, Sand and Stars*

THE Isle of Jersey, in the sun, can be a truly pleasant place. Sloping down from a high ridge on the north coast to a beach on the south, the whole island seems to have been deliberately tilted for the purpose of soaking up the sun's rays. Semitropical plants grow there, and enough tourists pass through to make its airport the third busiest in the United Kingdom.

But in a week-long rain, when you're trying to get somewhere else in a hurry, the place quickly loses its charm. Only ten miles long and six miles wide at the widest spot, it has one town and one village. It can be thoroughly explored in a day.

The crews of Mercy Missions had hoped to go on to Seville, Spain, on that first Monday. But the low black clouds through which they had descended soon settled right down to the ground. Visibility was zero, and takeoff was impossible.

They enjoyed a meal (and the Norman accents of the citizens) in the town of Saint Helier that night and used the enforced leisure to plan a redistribution of the cargo in John's plane. It had been uncomfortably tail-heavy on the trip down from Bovingdon.

The airport passenger lounge had been busy all day, filled with tourists whose outgoing flights had been canceled. Mercy Missions had received permission to sleep on the padded benches in the waiting room, but it meant that they had to wait until the last customer had gone back to his hotel before lying down. It was a restless night.

Tuesday morning was spent shuttling between the meteorological office, where the news continued to be discouraging, and the airmen's snack bar. Apparently they were trapped by the very same weather system that had held them at Bovingdon for four days; they had just followed it here.

John's crew solved the problem of tailheaviness by lashing all the cargo as high and as close as possible to the forward bulkhead, which divided the pilots' cockpit from the passenger cabin. This put the weight right over the wing. That afternoon there was a halfhearted attempt to keep busy by sweeping and dusting the aircraft, but no one's heart was in it.

The crew talked at dinner, and long into the night, about the lives they had led before starting this trip.

And then they bedded down again in the airport lounge.

Wednesday was a replay of Tuesday, except for a press conference John and Nick held at the request of some members of the posh Victoria Club to raise additional money for the trip. That night a member of the Aero Club invited the crew to sleep at his place, which turned out to be an enormous mansion on the hill overlooking the coast.

Thursday saw a few commercial planes come in during breaks in the weather, but no improvement encouraging enough for a takeoff. After a day of frustration and boredom, the crew found that their host of the night before was away on business, and that they could not sleep in the airport lounge that night either. Pilots of the incoming flights had joined a general strike against British Union Airways, and the lounge was filled with more than a hundred stranded passengers.

Painfully aware of how little cash they were carrying, the crew did not want to spend any of it on hotels. Most of them managed to wangle invitations to the homes of people they had met at the Aero Club, but Michael Draper spent a miserable night in a sleeping bag in the airplane. The plane was leaking again, after three days of continuous rain. And since it was a tail-wheel airplane, the floor of the fuselage was on a decided slant. Mike kept sliding downhill all night.

Friday morning brought the first hopeful forecast since their arrival. They laid out a course for their first stop, Bilbao, 350 miles to the south, stowed their gear in the planes, and haunted the weather office until four o'clock in the afternoon, when the meteorologist finally gave the go-ahead.

Nick put on his "uniform," since the next landing would be on Spanish soil and an official presence might be of some help. John made a quick inspection of the exterior of Mike-Golf; the others ducked quickly into the planes because it was still raining, though more lightly than it had all week.

At 4:30 they taxied to the end of the runway. Mike Draper noticed that the right wheel on Nick's plane seemed to be wobbling, but it looked to John like the usual unevenness of a tire parked too long in one place. They decided not to bother Nick with it, since he apparently was noticing no trouble with the wheel. Soon they were airborne.

Fifteen minutes of flying straight south, climbing all the time, brought them over the French coast. Visibility was still poor, and the clouds were full of ominous gray and black shadows. The weatherman had warned of a line of thunderstorms across the Bretagne peninsula, and the crew had no desire to end the mission by being torn apart inside one of those savage towers of wind and water. The powerful Jersey radar station had promised to keep track of them, however, and now told John and Nick which way to steer to pass between the storms. The radio was also continuously chattering with the calls of French pilots as they crossed the area, and the crews kept an anxious eye open for other traffic.

A little after 5:30, John looked down to see the estuary of the Loire River and the coast of the Bay of Biscay. As the Anson crossed the coast, it also broke out into clear, cloudless skies.

John radioed to Nick, in the other Anson eight miles behind, to tell him he had a beautiful afternoon ahead. And the crew relaxed to enjoy the beauty of the perfect sky, the ocean below and the French coast running parallel to their course for more than 200 miles.

Almost an hour later, halfway across the huge bay, Mike-Golf had its first emergency.

The crew first noticed a burning smell. Then the cabin began to get very hot. Fire in the air is a specter that haunts every pilot, and there was a frantic search for the source of the heat, which was becoming intense. Both engines were operating normally and their gauges were in the green, so it must be somewhere in the cabin. Ray began pawing frantically through the cargo.

It was Mike who discovered that the heat was coming from the cabin heating system. The heat control, on the right wall of the cockpit a little below his knee, had somehow been bumped into the "full on" position.

With the lever back to off, and the cockpit windows slid open so a gale of fresh air came blowing through, the plane quickly cooled off. But Mike found his briefcase too hot to pick up and, when he did get it open, found that his toothbrush had melted into a lump that looked like a piece of barley sugar.

Soon heart rates had slowed down to normal and the overheated baggage had cooled. But the incident had been a reminder to John and Mike that they still had a while to go before they really knew their airplane.

They already talked about Mike-Golf as they would about a living thing, and the affection they felt for her while they worked on her at Bovingdon was now growing while they flew. It was difficult to believe that it had been only a month since John had first seen her, baking in the heat of a crowded hangar at Bovingdon.

At that time she still had the RAF roundel like a target on each side of the fuselage. Her top was white and the bottom gray, divided by a two-inch band of deep blue running along the side.

There had been eight Ansons in the hangar. John and Nick had made their way slowly between the tangle of wings and fuselages, thumping the canvas, kicking tires and running fingers along the edges of the propellers. And three times different RAF pilots from the Communications Squadron on the base had come in, had seen what the men were doing, and had pointed to the Anson bearing the RAF registration number VV958. "Take that one," each man had said. "She's the best of the lot."

John took VV958. She was the T.21 model, designed to train navigators. There were seats in the cockpit for the pilot, a student radio operator and the radio instructor. Immediately behind them, through the cabin door, was a seat for the navigation instructor, facing aft. Thus seated, he could watch two student navigators, who sat at tables with their maps, protractors and slide-rule computers spread out before them. It was a flying classroom, with two teachers, three students and a chauffeur.

The logbook of VV958 showed that it had spent 4,707 hours in the air. In shuttling students back and forth across the British Isles from one practice checkpoint to another, she had flown more than 743,000 miles—nearly thirty times the distance around the equator. But she had never been outside the British Isles.

The log also showed that VV958 was nineteen years old and had worn out four pairs of engines. The current engines, according to the log, had another 800 hours of flying left in them.

Later John learned that VV958 was more than just the plane the RAF pilots had liked to fly best. She was literally the last Anson ever to fly for the RAF. In the

ceremonies on June 28, she had been the last of the
planes in the flyby, and thus the last to land. After the
ceremonies all the Ansons on the base had been parked
in Hangar Two and put up for sale.

On the same day that John had picked VV958, Nick
had chosen TX227. It had looked like a real war bird,
covered with irregular shapes of green and brown
camouflage paint. Mike, ever the air historian, tracked
down the fact that the paint had been applied by a
movie studio. TX227 had been recruited, along with
one other Anson, to play the role of a Dakota (the
RAF version of the American DC-3 transport) in
background scenes of the film, *Mosquito Squadron*.
The fact that a Dakota was half again as long and
had nearly twice the wingspan of an Anson did not
bother the studio.

Nick's plane was a Mark 19 Anson, designed to
carry passengers. It had six rather skimpy passenger
seats and a tiny toilet, all of which had been removed
in the conversion to civilian duty and its new name,
Mike-Hotel.

Now, 300 miles south of that hangar at Bovingdon,
the two Ansons were beginning the long descent
toward the Spanish coast. They could see the fashionable resort of Biarritz on the left, and on their right,
the setting sun and the ocean stretching away out of
sight.

The Spanish coast was mountainous and rocky; from
the air it looked like the geography-book pictures of
Scandinavian fjords. San Sebastián was easy to spot, but
John felt his way westward in the failing light for
twenty minutes before spotting Bilbao. They landed at
8:10 to find that Nick had taken a more direct
course and landed ahead of them.

Though the food that night was strange and not too tasty, Mercy Missions had an optimistic and happy crew. They were really on their way now, and the weather report for tomorrow was good.

Nick and Mike did a little sightseeing, but Mike found the poverty and the dirt of Bilbao depressing. Tony, the only member of the crew who spoke Spanish, had had a long hassle with immigration officials at the airport, who said the crew's papers were not in order. But he had convinced the officers that he would get the proper papers the next day in Seville, and they finally went away.

Most of the crew were glad to get to bed. But Nick Taaffe and Mike Draper, feeling suddenly the separation from home, sat up until two o'clock in the morning, talking about the girls they had left behind.

Sometimes, worn out by a day of flight, drenched in the humidity of the tropical climate, I have felt my heart beat in me like the wheels of an express train; and suddenly, more immediately than when flying, I have felt myself on a journey. A journey through time. Time was running through my fingers like the fine sand of the dunes; the poundings of my heart were bearing me onward towards an unknown future.

—*Wind, Sand and Stars*

EVERYONE but Nick was at the airport early the next morning, eager for the double hop to Seville and Casablanca. But when Nick arrived and began a hasty preflight inspection on Mike-Hotel, the good feeling disappeared. His starboard wheel, the one Mike had noticed wobbling the afternoon before, was in fact damaged.

A closer look by the two Johns showed that the wheel was broken and probably could not be fixed. If the Bilbao airport did not have on hand a right wheel for a Mark 19 Anson, one would have to be shipped from England. And that could take weeks.

John Smith made a collect call to the company that had sold the Ansons, and Bill Adams agreed to send the needed parts immediately by air express. But he pointed out that there were no direct flights from London to Bilbao, and he could not predict when the wheel would arrive.

After a long discussion, the crews agreed to split up. John Smith, Mike Draper and Ray Roberts would go ahead in Mike-Golf to get the airlift going. Anthony Stancomb would go along to make sure his film was finished as quickly as possible. John Desborough and Nick would follow when Mike-Hotel was flyable.

The transfer was quickly made. Tony didn't weigh much, but his camera equipment did. Some of the cargo was taken out of Mike-Golf to compensate for the weight, but the plane was still 200 pounds overweight on takeoff. They got off the ground at 12:20.

The flight to Seville was uneventful, though the strangely barren heart of Spain was a fascinating sight. They skirted the end of one 7,000-foot mountain range and forty-five minutes later had to climb to more than 8,000 feet to clear another range, the Carpetovetonica, which lay directly across their course. Just the other side of that range lay Madrid, and Mike was impressed by the number of bull rings that surround the capital, clearly visible from the air.

They landed at Seville at 3:50 in the afternoon, feeling the heat build up as they descended from the cool of 8,000 feet. It was 98° on the ground, the hottest temperature Mike Draper had ever experienced.

Tony, as promised, ran the passports into the Immigration hut while an efficient ground crew began the job of filling all six fuel tanks.

Later Tony discovered Mike inside the hangar with a flashlight, writing down the serial numbers of the different kinds of planes he found there—presumably for the next issue of *Blackbushe Movements*.

They were airborne again a little after 5:30, crossing huge olive plantations and then a series of salt-drying beds five miles wide and twenty miles long.

They crossed the coast at 6:10 and were thrilled to see Gibraltar on the horizon, far to the left. The coast slipped away behind them, and soon there was nothing in sight but the watery horizon.

That's when both engines suddenly quit.

It took only a second to realize that the auxiliary tanks in the cabin had run dry, and another second to switch the fuel feed over to the full wing tanks. But two seconds like that take several years off a flier's life. It was unanimously agreed that in the future the tanks would be switched at a preset time, *before* they ran dry.

After that, the rest of the flight was an anticlimax. The coast was under a cloud, and the Anson had to circle for a while to find Casablanca, but they were on the ground by eight o'clock, just a little after sunset.

Tony was the only one who had ever seen a city like Casablanca, so the crew decided to hire a taxi and tour the Arab quarter. They were disappointed to find that television had recently arrived in the Casbah. In every café and bar a fair-sized audience of Arabs had gathered to watch the shows—including, possibly on some late-night rerun, Humphrey Bogart and Ingrid Bergman in *Casablanca.*

Pilots like to say that flying is 95 percent boredom and 5 percent sheer terror. The next day's flight, a three-hour, forty-five-minute hop to El Aiún, fit that description.

It was Sunday, and the crew slept late. Takeoff was at 1:10 in the afternoon, with a minimum of fuss and red tape from the Moroccans. John headed west, out to sea, to get away from the bumpy air over land, and then set a course southwest toward El Aiún.

Soon after takeoff the crew had finished the usual housekeeping chores—straightening the gear in the cabin, adjusting seats and seat belt for the long ride, signing off from Casablanca radio and beginning to try to tune in the next radio beacon.

There was the usual chat about the takeoff, the weather ahead and the weather behind. A few reminiscences from the night before. Mike looked at the chart again, although he'd been memorizing it ever since Bovingdon.

Soon the talk tapered off. Up ahead, the towering cumulus clouds were building up, and the silent crew watched, wondering how rough it would be. To a casual passenger, the boiling energy of a pure-white cumulus cloud is a thing of beauty. But the airman in a light plane knows that each cloud is the top of a rising column of air, with updrafts of maybe 2,000 feet a minute. He knows he'll have to go beneath them, staying down around 5,000 feet where the heat is still bad, because he can't go over them. Most planes can't even climb as fast as the tops of the clouds can grow, reaching as high as ten miles in the air. Underneath, the pilot knows he will be bounced by the updrafts under each cloud and then sucked oceanward by the fierce downdrafts that flow between each cloud.

It isn't dangerous; it's just hard work. The plane makes better time if the pilot can hold it to one altitude, trimmed and "on the step" like a fast boat. Turbulence slows you down. It also can make your passengers airsick.

Out of habit, the crew continually searched the sky, looking for other aircraft. But this wasn't England, and if there were other planes here, they were lost in the hot blue of the sky and the deep blue below. Occasionally, Ray's eye would stop on the same fly speck on the windscreen, mistaking it for a plane far away on the horizon. Then he would complain to himself about the fact that when you're flying, you can't stop, get out and wipe the windscreen.

The seats were getting hard. They were not that soft in the first place—thin kapok RAF issue cushions on a steel seat. Tony was sitting on the bundles of emergency gear.

Four hours is long enough in a jet airliner, with "comfort engineered" seats and the right to get up and walk around if you don't mind crawling over two sets of legs to get to the aisle. But in a plane as small as an Anson, getting up and walking around means that you change the trim of the plane radically, making extra work for the pilot. In the case of Mike-Golf, Ray and Tony had to stay as close to the forward cabin bulkhead as possible because the plane was still a little tailheavy.

Mike, John and Ray were wearing headphones, and after twenty minutes these began to develop hot spots. The pressure of the phones clamped over one's ears for a long time produces a tiny area of intense pain on the ear, the temple or the jawbone. One phone can be slid back off the ear, keeping the other in place so the radio beacon beeping its identifier signal can be heard. But the phones are made to rest firmly, one on each side of the head, and when they are not worn that way they begin sliding and sometimes wind up in a tangle of wires on the floor.

It's impossible, of course, to take the headphones off completely. It's against all a crew member's training and experience; if he does remove them for a while, he is uncomfortable in the belief that he may be missing something, and he soon puts them back on.

There was nothing to see. After they had flown fifty miles over water, they had seen it all. They could look for the coast, but knew full well it would be another hour or two before it was close enough.

Ray, who had spent many an hour this way in Ansons and Shackletons, was beginning to settle comfortably into the old RAF routine. He opened the striped maroon-and-white thermos of coffee and handed a cup to John, with "Coffee being served, skipper." It had more than the ring of jest in it. It was the noncom attending to the needs of his commanding officer.

It was Ray who saw that the plane was kept clean and who stood by with John while the plane was refueled and the paperwork made out. He might grumble a little about the others not helping with housekeeping chores, but he obviously enjoyed the routine and the responsibility of doing it himself.

Mike had easily assumed his role, too. The old partnership with John, in which only a grunt or a nod or a pencil pointed to a spot on the chart was necessary for communication, had been reestablished as they learned to work with this airplane.

For Tony it was more difficult. He had the basic

footage for his film, barring some spectacular event en route, and now was waiting to get shots of the shuttle flights into Biafra itself. He had no radio to tune and no chart to watch. Often, on flights like this one, Mike would turn around to see him sound asleep on the cabin floor.

John had plenty to do as pilot, even on long dry flights like the one to El Aiún. But much of a pilot's work is unconscious; he doesn't think about doing it, and his mind has time to wander.

When John had first begun flying lessons, eighteen years before, flying straight and level like this seemed an impossible task, meant for athletes with lightning reflexes. When the instructor told him to keep his air speed at 100 knots and he concentrated on that, he soon discovered that he had gained 250 feet of altitude. He would watch the altimeter, and the instructor would bark that one wing was low.

Sweating and silently cursing, he would manage to get airspeed, altitude and wings into line all at the same time, only to be told that he had turned fifteen degrees off course. And by the time he had learned to juggle all these variables, each change in one affecting all the others, he was ready to learn how to get the plane back on the ground.

Every pilot has been through this. But now, like any other pilot with more than fifty hours in the air, John was not even conscious of the slight pressures on wheel and rudder pedals that kept the Anson exactly at 5,000 feet, pointed at 215 degrees, wings level, at an indicated 124 miles an hour.

At automatic intervals his eyes swept the instrument panel. First the flight instruments—airspeed, altimeter, rate-of-climb, compass, artificial horizon. Then the engine instruments, two of each, for the Cheetahs rumbling on each wing: manifold pressure, RPMs, cylinder head temperature, oil pressure, oil temperature, voltmeter, vacuum gauge, and the warning lights for low fuel and for generator failure.

The plane droned on. The Morse code identifying signal from El Aiún, a tiny settlement on the coast of Spanish West Africa, was all that could be heard in the earphones. Mike refolded his chart, to bring the next section on top, and saw that all the area now off to the left, over the horizon, was beyond the limits of reliable map data. It was plain white on the map.

Around 4:30 they finally saw the coast. It was Cape Juby, jutting out across their path, and "fantastic" was the word Mike used to describe it later. Waves of yellow ochre sand stretched as far as they could see ahead. It was divided from the dark blue of the sea by the thin line of white waves breaking on the beach. It was the first glimpse of the Sahara, and the effect was overpowering. There was little talk for a while.

Within twenty-five minutes they were within sight of El Aiún and descending toward a landing. The airport looked beautiful from the air, with a clean concrete runway and wide parking apron, and not far away, the picturesque little town.

John ended the long descent, banking the plane around into the airport traffic pattern, 800 feet above the ground. He edged the throttles forward for enough power to maintain that altitude.

That's when he noticed that the left engine was not responding the way it should.

To get the same power from the left engine as from the right, he had to move that throttle two inches ahead of the other. Something was seriously wrong, and the engine might quit any moment.

Very, very carefully he lined up the Anson with the runway and began the final approach. Not until he

371575

was within fifty feet of the ground and assured of hitting the right spot did he lower the gear; with the drag it created and with one bad engine, there would have been no chance of going around again.

But the landing was a good one. Mike and John slid open their side windows, and blasts of superheated air hit them. John grinned for a moment at Mike as they sat at the end of the runway, dead still, and then he began taxying toward the operations building, shimmering in the heat a half mile away.

7

Port Étienne is situated on the edge of one of the unsubdued regions of the Sahara. It is not a town. There is a stockade, a hangar, and a wooden quarters for the French crews. The desert all round is so unrelieved that despite its feeble military strength Port Étienne is practically invincible. To attack it means crossing such a belt of sand and flaming heat that the razzias (as the bands of armed marauders are called) must arrive exhausted and waterless.

—Wind, Sand and Stars

THE beautiful airport and the picturesque little town turned out to be the worst place any of them had ever seen.

It was so hot that breathing was difficult. The "hotel" to which they were directed was actually more of a bunkhouse; it was one big room with fifteen dirty beds. There were no other guests. There was no glass in any of the windows, and the flies and mosquitoes all seemed to live inside.

The hotel had a restaurant, and the hungry crew quickly dropped their luggage in the bunkhouse and went to eat. It was a mistake. The meal was not composed of anything recognizable, and it was served in a room dominated by the smell of an open sewer just outside the window.

Only Tony, the seasoned traveler, ate what was on the plate. "I thought it was rather funny," he said when describing it later to a friend, "being sort of a specialist in the atrocities of underdeveloped countries. But I'll admit it was one of the most sordid nights in a long time."

Mike was more emphatic. "It was the one meal of the whole trip that I had to just push away. I couldn't face it. You had the impression that by coming to this town, you were signing on for fifty years in the Foreign Legion."

There was no tap water, and they were afraid even to brush their teeth in the soupy liquid given to them in a bucket as water.

El Aiún, the airport manager told them when they went back to the airport that night, was one of only two towns in the whole country. He said Spanish West Africa covers 100,000 square miles—about the size of Nevada—and all of it is desert. It has roughly one resident for each of those square miles, mostly nomad Arabs and Berber tribesmen.

The manager seemed glad for company and put his mechanic to work on the troublesome engine. Meanwhile Ray soldered a loose wire in the intercom system, which had been cutting in and out all day.

The engine trouble appeared to be in the throttle linkage, and the mechanic soon pronounced it cured. The crew returned to their bunkhouse, determined to leave this place as early the next morning as possible.

Everyone was on hand by 7 A.M., after a night that had seen little sleep. But hopes for a quick getaway disappeared during the prestarting check when the left throttle jammed in a closed position.

John's inspection showed that the mechanic who "fixed" the engine the night before had put the throttle linkage back together wrong. He was able to fix it, and a long and careful check of the running engines showed that both could develop full power. They still required uneven throttle settings, but by now the crew's distaste for El Aiún was stronger than their concern for absolute safety. They took off for Dakar, where skilled mechanics should be available.

John stayed near the airport as he climbed to their cruising altitude, but by the time they reached 4,500 feet the throttles were operating the way they should. He turned southwest, following the coast to the first refuelling stop, Port Étienne.

It was the hottest leg of the trip so far. The cockpit, with its expanse of glass, was like a broiler. Everyone had his shirt off and sat as quietly as possible, wasting no extra energy. Mike found himself wondering whether he would ever see another cup of tea.

They followed the coastline over a different kind of desert than they had seen the day before. Dried-up rivers and salt lakes crisscrossed the area. Numerous miniature sandstorms looked from the air like little boys fighting. Twice the crew saw camel trains moving slowly across the barren land.

They found Port Étienne on Cape Blanco, a spit of land jutting out into the ocean. The landing approach brought them in over a small but busy harbor and onto a modern airfield, where they found the heat even more intense than it had been the day before at El Aiún. Even the goats, Mike noticed, found it an effort to move.

John had wired from Bovingdon the week before, requesting clearance to land here, and had received permission by return wire. But when the Anson came to a stop on the shimmering-hot parking apron, it was met by a pair of angry Army officers.

Tony, who had been concentrating on Spanish for the last three days, had to make a quick mental shift to French. It soon became clear that these officials knew nothing about the clearance and considered the Anson to have landed without one. And the confirming telegram had been left with Nick in Spain.

Tony turned on his most ingratiating manner and explained the situation. Not wanting to mention Biafra, he told the questioning officers that the plane was bound for Spanish Guinea. They wanted to know what a plane would do in Spanish Guinea, at which point Tony's knowledge of French conveniently deserted him again.

It took four hours to get fuel and a clearance to take off again. The stretch to Dakar, 420 miles, was a race against the sunset and a fight against sleep.

John, who not only had to fly every leg of the trip but also was responsible for most of the arrangements on the ground, was dead on his feet. He hadn't slept much the night before. And soon after the Anson had climbed to its cruising altitude, John found himself nodding.

He fought the urge for half an hour. Ray plied him with coffee and conversation. Finally he asked Mike Draper to take the wheel for a while.

Since there was only one set of controls, he had to crawl out of his seat and let Mike move into it. There wasn't much room to move around, which meant the transfer took time, so he took the plane up to 8,000 feet before making the change. The Anson went into a shallow dive while the wheel was untended, but it lost only about a thousand feet, and soon Mike, with his twenty hours' student experience, was coolly keeping the Anson on course.

John was back in his seat and the sun was just sliding behind the sea a couple of hours later when the Anson reached Dakar. The channel selector on the radio was refusing to work, so there was no way to get landing permission from the tower. John circled the airport several times, waiting for all other traffic to land or take off, before he set the plane down on the runway.

Now they were on the westernmost point of Africa, a major transfer point for the airlines, with most of the comforts of home. After El Aiún, the hotel they found at Dakar looked like the London Hilton. It was right on the beach and was surrounded by palm trees.

Flopping down on those clean white beds was one of the big thrills of the trip. But another high moment had come a little earlier, when they walked into the operations building at the Dakar airport. There on the wall was the big flight board, upon which was chalked a list of aircraft that had arrived that day. It gave each plane's ETA—estimated time of arrival, as furnished in advance by the schedule or the flight plan —and then its actual time of arrival. Making the actual time as close to the estimate is a matter of pride with airmen—a sign of professional competence.

The list included flights by Pan Am, Air Afrique, Air France and other big carriers. But on that day, August 12, only one plane had made its arrival coincide exactly with its estimate. It was written on the board in block letters, right up there with the rest: MERCY MISSIONS.

The crew was slow-moving, in no rush to get up the next morning. They finally arrived at the airport a little after ten. The intention was to fix both the radio and the throttle, which had been acting up again, and then fly on to Freetown, Sierra Leone.

But there were no mechanics available for hire, and the airline maintenance crews, who in most places had been friendly and helpful, couldn't be bothered with Mercy Missions.

Meanwhile Tony was having a spirited discussion with the airport authorities. After having paid an exorbitant landing fee for the plane and an airport tax for each passenger, he was being asked for another $10 for use of the runway lights.

Tony pointed out that they would have been only too glad to have had the lights, since it was dark by the time they got down without radio contact, but that nobody had bothered to turn them on. The Senegalese official insisted that the lights must have been turned on for anyone arriving so late and pointed to the arrival time still chalked on the big board.

Tony won the argument. But the crew soon decided it would be best to leave Senegal for a more friendly place. Tony and Ray began putting the cowling back on the engine. Mike went to get the weather report but was back soon to say that it would not be available until late afternoon. To start on a 450-mile trip across the African bush without knowing the weather ahead would be foolish, so they waited. Mike mentioned that several people had asked if they were going to Biafra; the Senegalese didn't seem to like the idea.

Everyone was fidgety and eager to get going by four o'clock, when they finally got the okay from the weatherman. The engines were fired and John called the tower for permission to taxi. "Stand by, Mike-Golf," was the answer.

Ten minutes later, when he called the tower to see if they had forgotten him, he got the same order to stand by.

Twenty minutes later the tower called: "You are cleared to taxi now, Mike-Golf."

"Thanks, Dakar Tower," John said. "What kept you?"

"Oh, nothing, Mike-Golf. When you reach Runway Three-Zero, hold short of the runway and we'll give you your takeoff clearance."

The Anson rumbled along the taxiway, John swinging its nose slowly back and forth so he could see any obstructions. When he came to the northwest-southeast runway, he performed the usual engine runups, and then called Dakar Tower.

"Roger, Mike-Golf, you're okay to take off now. Oh, by the way, what is your destination?"

"We're going to Freetown, Dakar Tower."

"Roger, Mike-Golf. And what is your ETA there?"

"About seven o'clock," John answered, "now that you've kept us waiting so long."

"Fine, Mike-Golf. Ah, stand by one minute."

They sat there a few minutes more in the damp, muggy heat of the late afternoon, the Anson's engines idling. Then the tower came back on the air:

"Mike-Golf, we've contacted Freetown. Of course, you're aware that if you take off at this time, you will be landing in darkness."

"Affirmative, Dakar Tower."

"Well unfortunately, Mike-Golf, Freetown will not accept your flight plan if you land after dark." There was a pause. "Have you an alternate destination?"

John and Mike were convinced by now that this delay was deliberate. They quickly spread out the map.

"There must be someplace on this map we can go," John said.

He punched the microphone button. "Dakar Tower, our alternate is Bathurst. May we take off?"

There was another pause. "Roger, Mike-Golf." The controller's voice was expressionless. "Cleared for takeoff."

Bathurst, Gambia, they soon learned, was only ninety-four miles away. The flight took just fifty minutes. When the crew landed, they were delighted to hear British accents and to discover that Gambia, a member of the Commonwealth, had an affection for anything English.

There was a warm welcome from the ground staff, including the chief fireman who had trained in England. The crew lazed away the evening with a swim in the warm, clean Gambia River, a good meal, and a visit to town. Tony ran into an old university friend from St. Andrews who took him to a party and, on the way back, turned the car over. Tony escaped without suffering anything except lack of sleep.

Peter Cadogan had left for Biafra two days before the Ansons had, taking a commercial flight to Lisbon and one of the airlift Constellations from there to São Tomé.

His job was to make all the necessary arrangements with the Biafran officials, including the commander of the Uli airstrip, for the Mercy Missions' planes to begin making regular landings. Hank Wharton, the pilot-of-fortune who operated most of the planes in the airlift, smuggled Cadogan through the Lisbon airport and onto the cargo plane. The next night Peter was on a flight that tried to go into Biafra but was turned back by heavy antiaircraft fire.

Finally on the night of August 5, the same date the two Ansons left England, Peter made it into the little flare-lit landing field inside Biafra.

There, helped by the excellent recommendations he had from Biafra House, he quickly negotiated the arrangements with the Foreign Secretary in Umuahia, Biafra's administrative center. George Nwanzi, the number two man in the Biafran foreign office, assured Peter of his full cooperation. He requested Mr. Jaggi, the Red Cross representative in Biafra, to notify the International Committee of the Red Cross on Fernando Po that they should release the secret landing codes to John Smith when he arrived.

Peter met Major Akaboju, who was in charge of transport, at the Uli airstrip. They made final arrangements together for the arrival of the Ansons.

It had been a hectic two weeks. The Biafrans had managed to retain all the worst features of the English colonial bureaucracy, multiplying the paper work and requiring everything to be done through convoluted channels. Even for would-be allies, the red tape required was inviolate—almost as though it were the one solid, unchangeable thing to which civil servants could cling amidst the chaos.

But when Peter left Biafra during the weekend of August 17, he was confident that all the red tape had been neatly tied up and that every possible obstacle to a smooth relief operation had been removed.

... War must be made to look like war. And nobody admits meanwhile that this war looks like nothing at all. That no part of it makes
sense. That not a single blueprint fits the circumstances. That the pup-
pets have been cut free of the strings which continue to be pulled.

—*Flight to Arras*

MIKE-GOLF would soon be making a very
long overwater flight to São Tomé, but her capacity for making long flights had not really been tested yet.

In Bathurst that night John proposed that the short-
est leg of the trip now be followed by the longest—a
563-mile leap across four other countries to Liberia.

This long jump down the coast would give the crew
a more exact idea of the Anson's range with the oil-
drum auxiliary tanks full.

Besides, they were eager to get to Biafra. They had
flown more than 2,000 miles. They had rounded the
hump of Africa, heading southwest all the time, and
now they were heading back toward the southeast and
their destination.

The rest of the crew agreed, and preparations began
early the next morning. It was like the planning for
any cross-country airplane flight, but the margin for
error this time was very small.

Mike got out the two big charts for the area covered
by this particular hop and matched them up on the
hangar floor. On his hands and knees, he drew the
course line straight from Bathurst to Monrovia. Then
he began marking off the line in twenty-mile segments
—about ten minutes' flying time at 120 miles an
hour. He looked for, and circled, features that would

make good checkpoints for determining ground speed. These had to be highly visible from the air and different enough that they could not be confused with other ground features nearby.

There were none of the features that show up so clearly when flying over England—racetracks, expressways, power lines and railroad switching yards. There were three railroad tracks—one in Guinea, one in Sierra Leone and one in Liberia. The first checkpoint, a "Y" in the Casamance River, would come after fifty-five miles of trackless swamp; the second, after sixty more of the same.

Mike also looked for obstructions—high towers or mountains—and made note of a 3,300-foot unnamed peak directly in their path 280 miles along the route in Guinea.

While Mike went to the weather office to find the direction and speed of the winds aloft, John was figuring the weight and balance of the Anson.

Using a plastic circular slide rule, he quickly figured that at 100 miles an hour (in case of a head wind) the flight would take five hours and forty minutes. At thirty-five gallons an hour, the plane would consume 200 gallons of fuel in that time. With auxiliary tanks full, the Anson held 220 gallons, so that part was okay.

Then he computed the weight of 220 imperial gallons of fuel at 7.2 pounds a gallon: 1,584 pounds. He added this, along with the weight of each crew member, the cargo, and thirteen gallons of oil (117 pounds) to the basic empty weight of the plane. The total was 500 pounds over the gross weight he was supposed to carry, but bush pilots often carried a much bigger overload. There was a safety factor built into that "allowable gross" figure, as long as one did not get too close to it or get caught in severe turbulence.

Mike came back from the weather bureau to report they would be facing a fifteen-mile-an-hour head wind, which was not so bad. By 11 A.M. the plane was refueled, loaded, checked for malfunctions, cleared by the airport authorities, taxied to the end of the runway and taken off over the swamps.

It was a routine flight except for thunderstorms two-thirds of the way down, over Sierra Leone. Turbulence tossed the plane around in up- and down-drafts that showed 1,700 feet a minute on the rate-of-climb indicator. But the Cheetahs had burned up 750 pounds of fuel by then, so there was no danger from overweight. And tropical thunderstorms do not form a solid squall line, as they do in northern climates, so the Anson could easily make its way between the worst of the storms.

As the Anson droned south over Senegal, Portuguese Guinea, Guinea and Sierra Leone, the crew was thinking more and more about Biafra.

For the first nine days of the journey, they had been fully occupied with the delays, with the mechanics of just getting from one place to another, with learning their jobs, and with the novelty and excitement of new places. But now, as they headed southeast, they began to feel their growing proximity to Nigeria, and to talk about the civil war.

All of them had been reading the papers and listening to the TV reports ever since they knew they were coming, and they had talked to pilots along the way who had been directly involved. They were beginning to see that the whole Nigeria-Biafra situation was much more complex than the general public realized.

Nigeria, in the bend where the rounded hump meets the tail of the continent, is Africa's most populous nation. In an area nearly twice as large as Spain, it has fifty-five million people—about the same as England, Scotland and Wales.

Until fifty-five years ago, it was a motley collection of pieces of land bought, stolen or conquered by English trading companies and eventually taken over by the British government.

It was in 1914, in order to present a stronger front against the Germans in nearby Cameroon, that all the pieces were merged by the British government into present-day Nigeria. (The name had been thought up by a lady correspondent of the London *Times* several years earlier.)

The merged colony, with its external boundaries arbitrarily drawn by treaty and by battle with the French and the Germans, lumped together three widely different and mutually hostile tribal groups.

In the north were the Hausa-speaking people, strongly Moslem, with a tradition of powerful tribal hierarchies. Their religious and temporal leader was the Sultan (or Sardauna) of Sokoto, who had the power of life and death over Moslems in the northern half of the colony and in the adjacent countries of Niger, Chad and Upper Volta.

The southern half of Nigeria was divided into two tribal groups. In the southwest were the Yorubas, with some 200 pagan gods, a smattering of Islam and some Christian influence. In the southeast were the Ibos and the Efiks, with smaller numbers of Ibibios, Kalabaris and Ijaws. These were small, hard-working, independent farmers. Instead of hereditary tribal rule, they had leaders who were elected and whose titles died with them.

Much of the blame for the war that happened later can be laid at the feet of Christian missionaries—many of them Irish priests of the Holy Ghost teaching order, and many of them Methodists from Great Britain.

As early as the appointment of the first British consul to the area, in 1849, the missionaries were establishing schools and trying to instill a desire for learning in the people. This is something that takes generations—old ways die slowly. But the Ibos came to have a tradition of eagerness to learn.

By the time mission schools were established in other parts of Nigeria, in the early years of this century, the Ibo people had a fifty-year head start on their countrymen.

The east was overpopulated; it never has been able to grow enough food for its own people. So some two million Ibos over the years took their learning and their skills to other parts of Nigeria, where they were successful in the professions, industry, commerce, the civil service and the Army.

Proud of their ability, they often struck the local Hausas or Yorubas as arrogant and boastful. And the local people, whose education had not prepared them for such choice jobs, were understandably jealous of the affluence and power of the alien Ibos.

Nigeria was granted its independence by Great Britain in October 1960, and at first it seemed to be off to a stable start. There were a well-trained civil service and a democratically elected government.

But the first president, Dr. Azikwe, was an Ibo. The people of the north, representing more than half the population, resented his leadership and the fact that the civil service was dominated and staffed by Ibos. There was frequent talk of secession by the north.

The government in each of the tribal groupings also became increasingly corrupt. Bribery was so common that businesses budgeted for it. Elections in all the regions were at times rigged or conducted under conditions of fear and coercion.

The shaky truce ended on January 14, 1966, when

five young majors of the Army captured Sir Abubakar Balewa, the prime minister, and killed the Sardauna of Sokoto and the premier of the western region. The prime minister died soon afterward in jail, probably from torture.

In Lagos, the capital of Nigeria, and in most of the southern half of Nigeria, there was public celebration over the end of the old corrupt government.

But acceptance in the north was mixed, because of the death of the religious leader of all the Moslems. And the five majors—three of them Ibos—had failed to secure control of the Army itself.

In the political vacuum that resulted, the five majors fled or were jailed, and the chief of staff of the Army, General Ironsi, was made head of state.

Ironsi, an Ibo, was not capable of ruling a country in such tension. While plans for coups and counter-coups were hatched, rumors swept the north that the whole revolution was an Ibo plot to take over the country.

(The arrogance of some Ibos did not help the situation; in one remote Moslem village 1,000 miles back from the coast, missionaries saw Ibos walking about the market, flaunting pictures of the dead and mutilated body of the Sardauna of Sokoto.)

The reaction in the north to the unrest and the rumors was the killing of several hundred Ibos in towns across the north.

On July 29 the fears resulted in another coup.

General Ironsi and the military governor of the west were stripped, flogged and shot. All Ibos in the Army, which included 75 percent of the officers, were dismissed. Forty-three officers and 141 enlisted men were put to death.

The senior northerner in the Army was Lieutenant Colonel Jakubu Gowon, Ironsi's successor as chief of staff. Now he became Commander-in-Chief and Head of State.

For two months Gowon seemed to be reestablishing trust in the government and demonstrating a measure of fairness toward the Ibos.

But exactly three months after Gowon assumed power, on September 29, 1966, a wave of mass killings of Ibos washed across northern Nigeria. John Bullock wrote in the *London Daily Telegraph* of October 22:

"In Kano, Kaduna, Jos, Zaria and a dozen other places the killings all began about 7 P.M. on Saturday. At each place the Hausa soldiers with loaded weapons were on hand, with gangs of young thugs imported from the surrounding countryside to help the troops. These groups were armed not only with sticks and machetes, but also with typed lists of addresses of Ibos. Hardly a spontaneous outbreak."

Radio Lagos, the government station, continually broadcast pleas to the Ibos not to flee, but to remain calm and to stay in their homes. But the killings went on, and by the thousands the Ibos picked up what they could carry of their possessions and tried to escape to the eastern region, their homeland.

Time magazine reported, on October 14, 1966, a typical scene:

The massacre began at the airport near the Fifth Battalion's home city of Kano. A Lagos-bound jet had just arrived from London, and as the Kano passengers were escorted into the customs shed, a wild-eyed soldier stormed in, brandishing a rifle and demanding *Ina Nyammari*—Hausa for "Where are the damned Ibos?"

There were Ibos among the customs officers, and they dropped their chalk and fled, only to be shot down in the main terminal by other soldiers. Scream-

ing the blood curses of a Moslem holy war, the
Hausa troops turned the airport into a shambles,
bayoneting Ibo workers in the bar, gunning them
down in the corridors and hauling Ibo passengers
off the plane to be lined up and shot.

More than one and one-half million Ibos fled to the
eastern region. But 30,000 were slaughtered before
they could get away, and at least three times that many
were injured.

(In Jos, all mail delivery stopped, because everyone
in the post office in this far northern town was an Ibo.
After a few weeks of ineffectual attempts by the Jos
town government to get the post office operating, missionaries began dropping in after work and sorting the
mail. They kept this up for months.)

The Gowon government made several attempts to
reach an accord with the increasingly isolationist and
fearful government of the eastern region. But, remembering Gowon's reassurances just before the massacres,
the Ibos could not bring themselves to believe that the
Federal government meant what it said—or, if it really
did, that it was able to enforce fair and just treatment
of Ibos by the aroused Federal soldiers.

The eastern region government, headed by Lieutenant Colonel Chukwuemeka Ojukwu, thought an
agreement had been reached at a conference in Ghana
to make of Nigeria a loose confederation. But this
agreement fell apart.

Soon afterward, in an attempt to bring the region
to heel, the Federal government refused to pay the
salaries due to civil servants in the region. The region
retaliated by retaining taxes due the Federal government. Lagos replied with a blockade of postal services,
and then of all land, sea and air transportation.

On May 26, 1967, the Consultative Assembly of

the eastern region voted to ask Ojukwu to declare the independence of the region "at an early practicable date."

General Gowon that same evening, and without prior announcement, decreed that the nation would be divided into twelve states forthwith. The eastern region was to become three of them.

Some observers saw this as an attempt by Gowon to reassure the Easterners—and to some extent the Yorubas in the western region—by cutting up the northern region, which was as large as all the others put together. Under the twelve-state plan, no state was large enough to dominate.

Others, however, including many Easterners, saw Gowon's plan as an attempt to separate the Ibo heartland, now known as the East Central State, from sections of the old eastern region, which did not have Ibo majorities.

Three days later, Lieutenant Colonel Ojukwu proclaimed "that the territory and region known as Eastern Nigeria, together with her continental shelves and territorial waters, shall henceforth be an independent sovereign state of the name and title The Republic of Biafra."

The area that seceded was roughly as large as Ireland and held more than fifteen million people.

Its new head of State, Ojukwu, was a millionaire's son. He was a graduate of Oxford, who refused to take over the family's banking and trucking interests, joining the Army instead. He was trained at Sandhurst, Britain's West Point, and had risen rapidly through the ranks. He had taken no part in the earlier coups and had been assigned as military governor of the eastern region not long before the massacres of his fellow Ibos began in the north.

Five weeks after the declaration of independence,

the Federal government set out on what it hoped would be a short, sharp police action. Ojukwu countered with a spectacular sweep to the west, driving the Federal troops back across the mid-west state, and into the western state, threatening the capital itself.

Ojukwu had reason for thus extending himself. The reason was oil.

About two-thirds of the known reserves of Nigerian oil at that time were located in the eastern region. The production is high; Nigerian oil accounts for about 10 percent of the United Kingdom's consumption. Ojukwu needed the oil for the economy of a small new nation and, if there were to be more fighting, to support an Army. He felt he had to show the oil companies he meant business and that a "police action" would not finish him off.

At first the oil companies continued to pay royalties to the eastern region. But it soon became obvious that the Federal blockade would be able to prevent shipping any of the oil out of the eastern region. When that became clear, the oil companies threw their weight and their considerable finances behind the Federal government.

Ojukwu had also hoped for moral support, at least, from America and from many other African governments that had recently earned their own freedom.

But America had too much prestige invested in the idea of Nigeria as a showcase nation. While the American public rooted for the underdog republic fighting for its freedom, the government and the business community pulled for stability and the recognized government.

And the African nations were frightened by the specter of "Balkanization"—the splitting up of many countries into tribal groupings. The fight of Katanga to break away from the Congo had ended not long before; members of the Organization of African Unity believed that if one breakaway state like Biafra succeeded, every nation would be plagued with the same problem.

The support did not come.

Meanwhile, Great Britain was supplying arms, ammunition, vehicles and military advisers to the Gowon regime. The sympathies of British people, like those of the Americans, were with Biafra. But Nigeria was a member of the Commonwealth, and there were major British business interests there, including Unilever, Barclays Bank and Portland Cement.

The Federal troops slowly began gaining back the lost ground. They took Port Harcourt and Calabar, the Biafran ports. They surrounded the Biafrans on the north, west, south and east, drawing the ring tighter.

By August 1968, when Mercy Missions was formed, Biafra was less than one-sixth the size of the old eastern region. Enugu, its capital, had fallen; once a city of 140,000 people, it was now a ghost town. As the circle tightened, the people, including many of the non-Ibo minority, kept moving in with it. Soon Biafra was a lop-sided circle less than eighty miles from east to west. And crowded into the area, without seaports, without the land to grow enough food for themselves, and without much future, were thirteen million people.

When the crew got into the thunderstorm area over Sierra Leone, talk about Nigeria stopped. John concentrated on maintaining altitude, and Mike and Ray on picking up the Monrovia radio beacon through the static.

During the worse siege, Mike looked back to see how Tony was faring. He was sound asleep, his long legs stretched out over the luggage.

They landed at 4:25 in the afternoon, after five

hours and twenty minutes in the air. Ray used the
Pan Am manager's desk to repair the VHF radio,
borrowing parts from the set they used least to make
the other one work.

They walked in the rain to the modern, American-
style motel at the airport, where they found the beds,
at $10 a night apiece, were far too expensive. But Ray
and Mike put on what Ray later called a "tremendous
charm campaign," before which onslaught the heart of
the manager melted, and he let the whole crew stay the
night free.

The machine which at first blush seems a means of isolating man
from the great problems of nature, actually plunges him more deeply
into them. As for the peasant so for the pilot, dawn and twilight become events of consequence. His essential problems are set him by
the mountain, the sea, the wind.

—*Wind, Sand and Stars*

IN Jersey the crew had met a pilot just back from
flying guns into Biafra.

"If the Nigerian jets catch you off their coast," he
had said, "they'll buzz you and force you to land. If
you don't land, they'll shoot you down."

Now, the closer they got to Nigeria, the more urgent
his advice seemed. It called, they felt, for a change in
plans.

They had already decided to fly southwest to São

Tomé, 300 miles south of the Nigerian coast, and then northwest to Fernando Po, which was only sixty-five miles off the coast. This dogleg would keep them well clear of the protruding Niger River delta.

But they had planned to make the overwater flight, some 500 miles, from Lomé, the capital of Togo. Now they were increasingly aware of the fact that Lomé was only ninety miles from the Nigerian border, and that a southwest course would take them within fifty miles of Nigeria.

They agreed, with very little discussion, to go directly to São Tomé from Abidjan, 315 miles west of Lomé.

Thus it was that, after a routine flight from Monrovia to Abidjan, they found themselves preparing for an overwater flight of 710 miles.

They needed another oil drum as a third auxiliary fuel tank and spent several hours attempting unsuccessfully to buy one. Finally they found a friendly oil-company manager, a French-speaking African, who told them he would look the other way while they stole one out of his warehouse.

The drum was strapped in place atop the two already in the cabin, leaving only a very narrow opening through which John and Mike and Ray could crawl into the cockpit. John planned to use fuel from the two auxiliary tanks for the first hour and a half, and then refill them by a hose from the new third tank.

The tank and fuel weighed around 350 pounds, which made the Anson nearly a thousand pounds overweight when she finally took off from Abidjan on the morning of August 16. It was 10:41 A.M. John used almost 7,000 feet of runway (instead of the usual 2,500) and lifted her off very, very gently.

They flew 6,000 feet, but it was still hot. This was a

different kind of heat than the desert's—much more muggy and oppressive. John had pulled back the cloth sunshades on the roof, in order to keep an eye out for the odd Nigerian fighter that might venture this far, and the sun beat down through the glass.

At 12:20 John gave the okay to begin transferring fuel from the third tank into the two permanent auxiliary tanks. In order to lessen the chances of an explosion, the radios and all other electric gear were turned off, and the cockpit side windows were slid open to blow away the fumes.

Tony had to siphon the fuel from the upper tank, which meant sucking on the hose until he got a mouthful of gasoline, then inserting the end of the hose in the filler hole of the lower tanks. The hose was small, and it took an hour and five minutes to make the transfer of fuel. Mike noted that the engines were burning the fuel just about as fast as it was being transferred.

At 1:31 P.M. Mike announced that they had just passed the point of no return; in case of emergency, it was now closer to go to São Tomé than back to Abidjan.

The engines droned on, and the plane seemed to be suspended motionless over the sea.

Soon after two o'clock Ray was able to tune in the first weak signals from São Tomé, and the radio direction finder showed that the Anson was exactly on course.

Cumulus clouds filled the sky now, and the Anson zigzagged lazily between them.

At 2:20 P.M. the two orange fuel warning lights winked on. The auxiliary tanks were empty. Mike quickly changed tanks, but the starboard engine sputtered a little bit before turning out full power again.

Now there was nothing to do but keep the radio-compass needle centered—and wait.

As the estimated time of arrival at São Tomé approached, they passed out of the area of towering cumulus clouds and found themselves atop a rolling broken layer of clouds, ranging in color from white to a deep gray, almost black. There was no sign of the island.

Mike fiddled with his time-and-distance slide rule, and Ray made occasional adjustments to the radio tuning knob. From time to time John would take his right hand from the wheel and, with thumb and forefinger at the base of one of the throttle levers, move it an unnoticeable fraction of an inch.

According to Mike's calculations, there were ten to twenty minutes of fuel left.

Then, slowly, the darkest of the gray clouds began taking on a shape more solid than the others. No one said anything. But in a few minutes it was obvious that this was the 6,000-foot mountain that dominated São Tomé.

John pressed the microphone button. "Ah, São Tomé, this is Golf-Alfa-Whisky-Mike-Golf, on a visual flight from Abidjan, ten miles out, requesting landing instructions."

"Roger, Mike-Golf," came the answer in a thick Spanish accent. "However, the ceiling here is only 300 feet, and we advise diversion to an alternate field."

John looked across at the map on Mike's knee. Fernando Po was 300 miles away, off the port wing. Cape Lopez, on the coast of Gabon, was 220 miles straight ahead. Those were the two closest pieces of solid land.

He told São Tomé, "Well, I think we'll give it a go anyhow."

The overnight stop at São Tomé turned out to be one of the most important of the whole trip.

They were taken immediately to see the Biafran representatives on the island, who gave them a warm welcome and assured them that all arrangements had been made for the shuttle of supplies. Later they met Father Byrne, the Irish priest who had done so much to wake up the world press about the hunger and misery in Biafra.

They also talked far into the night with the pilots of the airlift. There were several companies operating charter planes in and out of Biafra at that time, the most famous of which was run by an American, Hank Wharton. Wharton had four tramp aircraft, aging Constellations and DC-7s long since dropped from airline service in the USA, and half a dozen free-wheeling pilots to fly them.

Wharton's planes were available to anyone who could afford to charter them, which meant that a crew might take in rifle ammunition for the Biafran army one night and medical supplies for the World Council of Churches the next—though the flights were never mixed.

Wharton's pilots were full of advice on how to get in and out of Biafra unscathed, and the Mercy Missions crew listened intently.

They also met representatives of the World Council and of an organization called Norchurchaid, which was just beginning to make regular flights of food and medical supplies to Biafra. Founded by the Protestant churches of Scandinavia, Norchurchaid now was supported as well by Church World Service and Catholic

Relief Services, American church relief organizations; by Caritas, and by the World Council.

One of the Norchurchaid pilots let John copy the complicated radio codes that he needed in order to land at the tiny, hidden Uli airport in Biafra without being shot down by the Biafrans themselves.

On Saturday morning they pulled the wheel chocks from in front of Mike-Golf for the last leg of the long journey. It was still rainy, and Mike went off for a final check of the weather while John was doing the exterior inspection. Tony took a closer look at one of the charter DC-6s on the field; it was covered on the inside with maggots and bugs and on the outside with leaking oil.

As the crew got ready to climb aboard, a young American, red-eyed and unshaven, approached John and asked for a ride to Fernando Po.

Ray, just out of earshot, remarked to Mike: "What on earth is this junkie doing here?"

The man identified himself as Charles Bailiff of Church World Service. He had been on his way to an assignment in the Central African Republic, he said, when he had been told instead to go to Fernando Po temporarily as World Council of Churches representative.

"Terribly sorry," John said. "We're over our legal weight already."

The crew had no way of knowing, as the Anson pulled away and left him standing by the runway, that Bailiff's rather dubious appearance was the result of four days of air travel, most of it without sleep. Or that he was an attorney with a doctor's degree in law.

Or that he would one day save them all from prison —and probably from being hanged.

Almost immediately after takeoff the Anson was in the low clouds. John climbed up through to the sunlight, and the Anson sped along just above the tops of the clouds.

They never saw the Portuguese island of Principe, but they knew they were passing directly over it by the movement of the radio-compass. It came earlier than expected; obviously they were enjoying a strong tail wind.

At 4:30 the dial indicated they had passed Fernando Po. John descended cautiously through the clouds, breaking out at about 500 feet into a hazy drizzle. Visibility was so bad he had to continue flying on instruments. Mike had to watch the boost control and the throttle, which still were not functioning correctly.

So it was Ray who stood between them, peering out into the mist, and who suddenly shouted, "Cliffs ahead, turn left now!"

John banked sharply, and then followed the vaguely visible coastline of the island around to the airport on the northwest corner.

The occasion, they agreed as the Anson settled to the runway, called for a celebration. It had taken thirteen days, including forty hours of flying, to get here. But finally they were ready to fly into Biafra.

Or so they thought.

An administration is a machine. The more perfect the machine, the more human initiative is eliminated from it. . . . But a machine is not built for creation. It carries on. . . . An administration is not conceived for the purpose for solving fresh problems. . . . An administration is conceived as a safeguard against disturbances resulting from human initiative.

—*Flight to Arras*

IT seemed to John that the first thing they should do, after a good dinner and a bath, was to announce their presence to the local representative of the International Committee of the Red Cross.

The ICRC had agreed to store not only its own supplies, but also supplies sent to Fernando Po by Oxfam, the British relief agency, and by the World Council of Churches.

Before Mercy Missions had left England, the crew had been told that if the Ansons actually got to Fernando Po, Oxfam would consider using them to carry its supplies.

Charles Bailiff had said the same thing on behalf of the WCC, the day before on São Tomé. The WCC, he said, had seventy-one tons of medical supplies and food on the island.

The ICRC staff had been sharply cut back since the suspension of flights on August 9. But John found the address of the representative now in charge, a Swiss named Stegerman, and set out at ten o'clock at night to find him.

The rest of the crew, eager to get going and envisioning the possibility of a Biafra flight in the morning, insisted on going too.

When Stegerman came to the door of his rented villa, he was hopping mad, and in his pajamas. He had been asleep, he said, and did not appreciate being awakened.

He had known that Mercy Missions was coming, he added, and would deal with its crew in the morning.

The crew was at breakfast in the hotel the next morning when Stegerman, now fully dressed, came in and sat down at their table.

He accepted their apologies for waking him the night before, and then abruptly announced, "I cannot release to you any of the food in our warehouses. Your whole operation is highly irregular."

He said he had been in touch via cable with Dr. Auguste Lindt, the ICRC Special Commissioner for Nigeria-Biafra, and that Dr. Lindt agreed with the decision.

Mercy Missions perhaps had good intentions, he said, but their plans were foolhardy. The Red Cross would not and could not be a party to their suicide.

The crew sat there, stunned, their breakfasts unfinished.

In any event, Stegerman went on, the little Ansons were so insignificant as to be ridiculous. They would only clutter the air over the Uli landing strip.

When he had finished, there was silence from the crew. Finally John spoke. What about the Oxfam and WCC food, he asked. Surely the Red Cross had no objection to their flying that in.

All the 3,000 tons of supplies in the Red Cross warehouses, Stegerman replied, were under his jurisdiction. He would release none.

Quietly, John began to argue Mercy Missions' case.

First, they would be flying in the daytime, when there were no other relief flights going in, and thus could not cause congestion over Uli.

Second, they could make three or four flights a day to areas where the DC-7s could not land, saving much of the fuel now expended on ground transportation.

Third, ICRC would be absolved of any responsibility for the crew's "suicide." In any event, the Ansons would be going in low, under the Nigerian radar, and would actually be in less danger than the night flights were.

But the Swiss remained adamant. He excused himself and stalked out of the hotel.

(Months later, Ray was asked what the crew's reaction had been to this announcement. "Disbelief," Ray said, "turned to fury. Turned to rage. Turned to despair.")

John and his crew went back out to the airport, where they met pilots and mechanics of an English firm, Bristow Helicopters. This reunion of Englishmen helped them forget their disappointment for a moment, especially when the helicopter people produced something the crew had not seen in nearly two weeks: a hot cup of English tea!

From the control tower, they were able to send a message to Father Byrne in São Tomé, advising him of their predicament. Then they passed the rest of the day and the evening trying to decide what to do.

John never had felt so helpless. Communications were difficult; the Red Cross controlled the only teletype on the island, and they had no money for international phone calls. There was no one to whom they could appeal on the island. There really was nothing they could do except get the Anson ready and wait for Father Byrne or Charles Bailiff to order the release of some cargo.

It was not until much later that the crew pieced together all the reasons why the Red Cross had stopped its flights and was now refusing to release relief supplies to Mercy Missions. But basically it was the ICRC's insistence on working only through recognized governments.

Nigeria was a recognized government; Biafra was not. The ICRC officials in Lagos, usually Swiss businessmen on their thirty-day holidays and in Africa for the first time, were not in a position to evaluate the complications of the war. Living in the best air-conditioned European hotel, resplendent in newly tailored uniforms, they were subjected to a continual barrage of pro-Nigerian thought.

The ICRC headquarters at Geneva, under terrific public pressure to help Biafra, was facing even more powerful pressure *not* to do so. The Organization of African States was on record as deploring anything that would help the Biafran cause and thus contribute to the breakup of a sovereign African nation. The British government stood squarely with the Nigerians, and many of its officials could be heard expounding the quick-kill theory—that relief to Biafra was only prolonging the agony and condemning more children to death.

The Nigerian ambassador to the Netherlands, Mr. Durlong, gave some indication of the Red Cross's relationship in an interview with the Dutch paper *De Tiyd.*

"We started with a number of disagreements with the Red Cross. Now we believe that all relief organizations must channel their activities through the Red Cross."

Referring to the Norchurchaid airlift from São Tomé, he added, "It is not clear to me why the relief organizations won't work together with the internationally recognized Red Cross."

The Dutch interviewer suggested, "Perhaps because the Red Cross is a supporter of the quick victory of the Federal government?"

"I believe indeed," the ambassador said, "that the Red Cross is a supporter of a quick victory by the Federal government."

There was American pressure against aid to Biafra, too, and this figured in the Red Cross's dilemma. While the USA was officially neutral in the civil war, the Assistant Secretary of State for African Affairs, Joseph Palmer, was strongly in favor of keeping Nigeria together as a nation. Palmer once called American relief officials to Washington mainly for the purpose of lecturing them on the fact that there was no such thing as Biafra and that the word should not be used.

Officials of such groups as the American Friends Service Committee, Catholic Relief Services and Church World Service had long pled with the US government to release a Hercules turboprop cargo plane, which could haul thirty-five tons of cargo on each flight—three and one-half times the capacity of a DC-7. Eventually they were told they could lease such a plane—but only if the ICRC controlled where and how it would be used.

The other relief groups, aware of the ICRC's vulnerability to government pressure and its ties to Lagos, refused the offer.

An article by Lloyd Garrison in *The New York*

Times Magazine of that period helps clarify America's role behind the scenes in supporting Nigeria:

The U.S. and Britain saw in an independent Nigeria the makings of the most populous, most powerful, most democratic of all African nations. Nigeria, it was proclaimed, would become a Western showcase, a Communist-free bastion thriving on huge injections of Western aid and Western free enterprise.

The chief architect of the "showcase" Nigerian policy was Ambassador Joseph Palmer, an able, sensitive career diplomat who is now Assistant Secretary of State for African Affairs. . . . With Palmer's promotion to Washington, the "showcase" policy became gospel for American diplomats.

Whether the cause was politics or an honest belief in the quick-kill theory, it was obvious that the ICRC's relief flights into Biafra were sporadic, and by August 9 had stopped completely. (This was at the height of the Federal offensive against Aba and Owerri, a campaign that was to have signaled the end for Biafra.) The date, September 15, cropped up frequently in conversations in London, New York and on Fernando Po as the date when flights might be resumed—although this was never said publicly. And September 15, critics of the ICRC pointed out, was the date by which most experts believed the last Biafran cities would have fallen.

There was one major flaw in the quick-kill theory, and the crew of Mercy Missions soon learned about it on Fernando Po. The theory presumed that the Nigerian government would, as General Gowon promised, give full cooperation to groups providing relief to the war-ravaged areas after the fighting stopped. But on Fernando Po there were people who had seen the large Ibo areas that the Federals had retaken from Biafra more than a year earlier. They knew that the Federal government was still preventing relief teams from helping, or even entering, many of these areas.

The concern for the innocent victims of the war, expressed so loudly in advancing the quick-kill theory, was very feebly expressed in the areas Nigeria was already holding.

(John went to see the Nigerian consul on Fernando Po the second day he was there, offering to alternate the Biafra flights with flights to any refugee area of Nigeria. After a week of stalling, the consul reported that permission was granted—but only if Mercy Missions would first stop at Lagos on every flight, including the Biafra ones! Later even this offer, unacceptable as it was, was withdrawn because of "the pressure of paper work in Lagos.")

It was a Sunday morning, August 18, when Mercy Missions got the shocking news that they would be refused a cargo. But during the next three days came some of the most significant activity of all the crew's efforts. Because by Thursday night, the Red Cross was flying again, and Mercy Missions was the main factor in bringing it about.

The crew had gone to the airport early on Monday to work on the Anson. They arrived just in time to meet a young English doctor who was disembarking from an Iberia Airlines plane, along with his assistant and two nurses.

He introduced himself as Dr. John Wallace of the British-based Save the Children Fund. His team had been sent to work in Biafra, and they were counting on flying in that same night with the Red Cross relief plane.

A deceptively frail-looking young man with nervous energy to spare, Wallace was disturbed to learn from John that the Red Cross had quit flying. "How will I get into Biafra?"

"Don't worry," said John. "We'll fly you there tomorrow morning." He made arrangements to meet with Wallace later in the day.

Then they got busy in the Anson. They dismantled the two big auxiliary tanks and rolled them away. The carpeting, the store of spare parts, the one useless radio and anything else that added unnecessary weight were removed.

When they saw Dr. Wallace again, he had already talked to Stegerman. The ICRC man had offered no hope of a Red Cross flight, he said.

That evening both Ray Roberts and Dr. Wallace sent out cables with a pilot departing for Lisbon; they would be sent from the Lisbon office. Ray's messages were to the Sunday *Times* and the *Express*, reporting the Red Cross refusal to supply food for Mercy Missions. Dr. Wallace's message went to his organization's headquarters in London and the ICRC in Geneva, complaining of the refusal to fly him to Uli.

Mike, meanwhile, was spreading the word around the airport of Mercy Missions' friendly relationship with BBC-TV. The *Twenty-Four Hours* news team was expected on the island any day, and Mike predicted great waves of shock and horror when the British public found out why Mercy Missions wasn't flying.

On Tuesday, about midmorning, the crew noticed that the one remaining Red Cross plane was being loaded, as if for a trip. And that night it did go, indeed, to Biafra, with Dr. Wallace and his helpers aboard.

There still had been no answer from Father Byrne in São Tomé, so the crew continued to work on the plane. And during the afternoon on Wednesday, Charles Bailiff finally arrived.

Bailiff had had some rest and food, and looked quite different from the "junkie" Ray had seen at the São Tomé airport. A slender, sandy-haired chain smoker, Bailiff was well qualified to step into the confused situation at Fernando Po. He had been around. While working toward his doctorate in law, he had worked for a detective agency, had been a clerk-typist at the FBI headquarters, and had served a year as assistant to a Congressman. He had been secretary of the American Law Student Association of the American Bar Association, and had spent the last two years with the Peace Corps in Togo. He had studied at Baylor, George Washington University, the University of Alabama, and the University of Paris.

His goal had been to enter politics in Florida, his home state. But his successful fund-raising for Biafra in the St. Petersburg area had brought him to the attention of Church World Service, who needed a man to work with Sudanese refugees in the Central African Republic. He had immediately agreed, when approached by CWS, to postpone politics for a few years and go to Africa.

Now he had been sidetracked again, sent by CWS and by the World Council of Churches in Geneva to see why food wasn't moving out of Fernando Po.

It was a memorable evening, which began with a retelling of the woes caused by Stegerman, and ended up in a party at the Fisherman Club, hosted by John and Marjory Chapman, a missionary couple they had met.

Charles went the next morning to confront Herr Stegerman, but came away no more successful than

John had been. The ICRC man not only refused to release the WCC food to Charles, he refused even to accept Charles' letter of introduction. The situation was in hand, he said, and Charles' presence was not required.

Later Charles visited a Red Cross radio operator he had met the night before. The man, who spoke only French, was very friendly and agreed to send a radio message to the World Council of Churches in Geneva. The message Charles handed him was in English, and the poor man never knew what he was sending.

But when it landed in Geneva it caused an explosion. Copies were quickly cabled to Church World Service in New York, and a Catholic Relief Services copy turned up on the desk of Dr. Lindt at ICRC's Geneva headquarters. Anger and consternation was the reaction each place.

The message merely reported the facts, which Fernando Po's poor communications might otherwise have kept from the outside world for weeks: that the Red Cross was not making relief flights, was refusing to release supplies contributed by other groups, and was refusing cooperation with other groups.

The cumulative effect of that message—the threat of TV exposure, Mercy Missions' offer to take Dr. Wallace to Biafra if the Red Cross would not, and Ray's messages to the London papers—was soon felt.

The Red Cross began sending its one plane to Uli every night, and there were reliable reports that more planes were on their way to Fernando Po. A Hercules operated by the Red Cross arrived the following Tuesday, bringing with it two ambulances and a dozen relief workers. And Dr. Lindt himself arrived in his private propjet to see what all the fuss was about.

All this meant that the Red Cross was moving, but it didn't help the frustrations of the Mercy Missions crew. These frustrations were being multiplied, in fact, by a first-hand look at the horror created by the civil war.

Many of the people they talked to in the market at Santa Isabel or along the coast were Ibo tribesmen who had fled Nigeria in wooden canoes. With their instinct for trading, they were managing to make a living. But the stories of their persecution in Nigeria troubled the crew.

They told of hiding out in the bush without food while Nigerian soldiers thrashed about, swinging machetes or spraying the scene with submachine gun bullets. They told of being overrun twice by fighting—first by the Biafran troops claiming both the eastern and the midwest regions, and then by Nigerian troops counterattacking. One old man told the crew he had watched 150 young Ibos lined up beside a trench and gunned down. The trench had become their grave.

In the areas recaptured by the Nigerians, the refugees said, no relief food or medicine were allowed to get through. The hospital at Calabar, months after the recapture of that port city, was still not in operation.

And all the refugees talked about the hunger. The stories were true, they said. People on both sides of the lines were dying because the war had churned up the fields or killed the sowers of seed. All the fall harvest was gone, and people were eating the yams they should be using for seed for next year. One mother told of seeing little children sitting by the road in rows, too weak to move, staring silently until, one by one, they fell over and died.

For the crew, this was a new and disturbing look at something that had been just statistics before.

They had known there was a problem; basically, that was why they had come. But talking to people who had been there brought the terrible horror of it home. The youngster they had seen in the market, with her legs permanently bent by the malnutrition and one arm just a stump because of a bomb fragment—that youngster might have been John's three-year-old Sennen-Dee. The graceful young woman trying to fish from a leaky log canoe in order to feed her crippled mother looked the same age as Carol, Mike's girl back in the bank.

These encounters deeply moved the crew. They went to Bailiff again. "Can't you do something," John asked, "to get us cargo for Biafra?"

This time Bailiff could. He had cleared with his superiors in New York the idea of chartering an Iberian cargo plane to bring five tons of supplies for Mercy Missions from São Tomé. This would keep the heat on the Red Cross, he figured, as well as making use of the skills and motivation of the crew.

Of the latter, Bailiff had a high opinion. He wrote that week to a Church World Service official in New York:

Of all the people I've met along the way, I'd have to say that these men are 150 percent dedicated to saving the Biafran children.

They are paying their own way (so far all donations have gone toward payment for the planes, their maintenance, petrol and incidental necessities), eat only one meal a day, and exude so much guts in being willing to brave the antiaircraft and risk daytime flights that, as Rev. Thompson says, "One can't help but be impressed with their wealth of spirit and character from the moment of one's first encounter."

Meanwhile, the crew had been worrying about Nick, too. Even allowing two weeks for the spare wheel to arrive and be installed at Bilbao, Nick and John should have been here by now.

The second plane was important as a back-up in case anything went wrong with Mike-Golf. With a second plane, an accident or trouble in Biafra would not be disastrous; they could keep the operation going.

Communications were difficult, of course, and neither they nor Nick had money to spare for cables. So they just worried and wondered.

The word came one sultry evening in the last week in August. One of Wharton's pilots, just in from Lisbon, brought a wrinkled envelope addressed to John.

The note had come from Nick in Port Étienne, hand-carried by friendly pilots south to Dakar, then back up to Lisbon.

John read the note, his shoulders sagging, then handed it to Ray and Mike without a word.

The fractured wheel, the note said, had been quickly shipped by Alec Dowse and had been efficiently installed by the Spanish mechanics. Mike-Hotel, heavily loaded and with Nick and John Desborough aboard, had then followed the path of Mike-Golf—to Seville, Casablanca and El Aiún.

On the third day, following the coast of Spanish West Africa where the Sahara pushes right out to the sea, they had run into a sandstorm.

They had seen it coming, fifty miles away, a wall of deep brown that rose 20,000 feet into the air. It was higher than the Anson could climb and stretched on their left to the heart of the Sahara. Somewhere inside it was the cluster of huts and an aerodrome that make up Port Étienne.

They knew, too, that as strong as the Cheetah

engines were, they wouldn't run very long on a diet of sand. A big knobbed lever just left of center on the instrument panel could move a filter in front of the carburetor intakes, but in minutes the sand would pile up against the filters and clog them, cutting off air to the engines.

Leaving the air cleaners out of the way meant that the sand, like pumice, would soon be scouring the insides of the cylinder walls and the bearings.

For the moment, however, Nick's main worry was finding the aerodrome. Fortunately, the radio beacon was coming through loud and clear, and the crossed white needles on the direction finder dial held steady, urging him straight ahead.

There was little choice. There wasn't fuel to go back to Villa Cisneros, 150 miles behind. It was land on the beach, hoping you missed the soft spots and that somebody would find you before the heat finished you off, or keep on probing ahead for Port Étienne.

The Anson plunged into the wall of sand. Sky, ground and horizon were blotted out. The artificial horizon, a three-inch dial on the instrument panel, and the direction finder were the only reality. But the engines droned on.

Fifteen minutes before their ETA at Port Étienne, Nick and John Desborough were already leaning forward, noses to the windscreen, searching for a sign of the airport. Gradually they were losing altitude, hoping to see the coastline well enough to follow it in.

That's when the port engine coughed, shook and quit running.

Without thinking, Nick ran through the feathering procedure for that engine: close the throttle, slam the RPM lever down into feather position, lift the safety cover and jab the feathering pushbutton on the panel, switch off the ignition, cut off the fuel, jam the throttle on the good engine forward to "climb power."

He knew, with nearly a ton of overload and in the thin, hot air, he could not maintain altitude on one engine. John was just unbuckling his safety belt to go back to try to jettison some of the cargo when Nick shouted, "There's the place!" Dimly, straight ahead, they could see the beacon.

Gingerly, Nick began the normal circuit around the strip, knowing that if he misjudged his landing there would be no chance to go around. With the port engine dead there was only enough hydraulic pressure to lower the flaps; John lowered the landing gear with fifty laborious strokes of the emergency hand pump. The plane swung around onto final approach. Nick's leg was beginning to tremble from the effort of holding the left rudder nearly all the way forward, balancing the lack of power on that side.

As they felt their way down through the murk, they could see that sand had drifted across the runway in great piles. But there was nothing to do but keep going down. The starboard engine might quit any minute.

When it was clear that the plane would touch down on the right spot, near the approach end of the runway, Nick reached around behind him on the right and held down the flap lever. The plane sank more rapidly, Nick raised the nose slowly, and with a "chirk" that was almost inaudible behind the roar of the engine and the howl of the storm, the wheels touched the ground.

But before he could relax, one of the shifting piles of red sand was directly ahead, nearly as high as the wing. The starboard wheel hit the dune, and the plane swung to the right, careening off the runway.

Nick couldn't see what was ahead—buildings,

parked airplanes, people, or what. But if there were
any of those things, he had to stop the plane fast.
Reaching down beside his right knee he flipped the
safety catch aside with his thumb and jerked straight
up on the landing gear knob.

With a sickening thud and a screech the Anson
folded up its wheels and settled to the ground, coming
to a stop against another sand dune.

By the time the airport attendants had groped their
way out through the storm to see how bad the damage
was, Nick had already made a complete check. Neither
man was hurt. The starboard propeller, still running
when the gear folded, was ground to a stump. The
port propeller had originally come to a stop straight
up and down, so the bottom half, sticking down, had
been snapped off cleanly. The Pitot head, a three-inch
length of tubing sticking forward from one wing to
measure air speed, was bent.

Nothing else on the airplane had been hurt.

But it would be weeks before they could get another
prop from Bovingdon (they had one spare aboard)
and get going again.

The news from Nick was a real blow. But the news
from São Tomé was good. After a hassle with the
Spanish authorities over whether customs duties ought
to be paid on the incoming supplies, all arrangements
were completed and an Iberia Airlines plane arrived
with a cargo of dried milk and egg powder.

The crew spent Saturday afternoon loading nearly
two tons of the food into the fuselage of Mike-Golf,
piling it as far forward as possible. They filled the
fuel tanks, checked the air pressure in the tires,
patched a bit of loose canvas on the underside of the
tailplane. (Iberia mechanics had fixed the port engine,

and a test flight had shown the throttle to be operating perfectly.)

John and Mike went over the chart once more, remembering the advice of Wharton's pilots about the best routes.

And then they went to bed, planning on an early takeoff the next day for Uli airstrip.

I did not come at once upon the firing line. In a civil war the firing line is invisible; it passes through the hearts of men.

—Wind, Sand and Stars

SUNDAY, September 1—the start of a new month and, the crew felt, the start of a whole new cricket match. The sky was clear; even the little wreath of clouds that usually hung around the tip of the mountain was missing.

Mike-Golf had been waiting, cargo aboard, fuel tanks full, since yesterday. By 9:30 A.M. everyone was on board.

The crew for this trip were John, Mike and Ray. This wasn't the way it originally had been planned; Mike had signed on for the trip with the understanding that he would go only as far as Fernando Po.

But that was back in Camberley—a decision made by a young student pilot who had never been farther away from home than Paris. Two things had happened in the meantime to make him feel differently: Since then he'd flown more than 4,000 miles with this crew in every kind of difficulty, and he had met the Ibo refugees from Biafra.

Now he not only was willing to go, he insisted. John, he argued, would have his hands full at low altitude just flying the plane. Ray would be busy with the radio. He, Mike, was needed to keep the charts, figure the groundspeed and know their exact position at any minute. This was no place to get lost.

John had to agree, although Mike's weight would mean they could carry one less 100-pound sack of milk powder. So when they started engines, Mike was in his usual spot, at John's right and a little behind, the earphones clamped over his shock of red hair, the air charts on his lap.

As they taxied to the runway, they could see Tony, a lonely figure, following them through the viewfinder of his movie camera.

John had filed a flight plan for Libreville, the capital of Gabon, 200 miles south-southwest of the island. No use broadcasting their true plans. So as Mike-Golf lifted off the runway, at 9:45 A.M., John asked the Fernando Po tower for permission to make a right turn out of the airport pattern.

"Right turn approved, Mike-Golf," the voice came back.

Then, after a moment: "Oh, Mr. Smith?"

"Yes, Tower?"

"Uh, Mr. Smith, my wife likes flying very much. And I like to fly also. Do you suppose when you come back, you could give us a little flight around the island?"

"Of course," John replied. "We'll give you a flight when we get back."

And the crew of Mike-Golf set off for the guns of Nigeria.

They continued southeast until out of sight of the island, and then swung around to the left, toward the Cameroon coast. Mount Cameroon, 13,300 feet high, loomed above them even when they had completed their climb to 5,000 feet. Ray reported he had picked up the Kano radio beacon, and they turned once more—toward the northwest and Biafra.

It was a marvelous day to be flying. At 5,000 feet they were out of the heat. They could see little boats, and once a freighter on the deep blue water below. Twenty minutes after they made their final turn they saw the coast—a faint white line against the blue.

John throttled back and let the Anson glide, her engines barely ticking over, until she was skimming just above the sea. Then he fed in the power again, and the waves blurred as they roared along, thirty feet above the water, at 120 miles an hour.

They hit the coastline at Uquo, about five miles west of their intended landfall. John turned left and followed the wide, white beach. There were people on the beach, some of them cooking meals; they looked up from their bonfires and waved.

There wasn't a gun in sight. There wasn't even an unfriendly gesture from the people looking up at them. Mike remembered the mental picture he'd had of a blazing sky full of exploding rockets, and grinned.

At the mouth of the Kwa Ibo River, John banked steeply to the right and began following the river. This was a safety zone known to all the pilots going into Biafra; for five miles each side of the river the land was too marshy to support antiaircraft guns.

It wasn't jungle, but it wasn't open country either. There were plenty of trees, scattered but just close enough, from a pilot's point of view, to keep it from being good forced-landing country; there was no open space big enough to set even an Anson down without losing a wing against the trunk of a palm.

They were at fifty or sixty feet; "Just above the palm trees," Ray remembers, "and sometimes I think we brushed a treetop."

Ray was the lookout, watching for Nigerian Mig fighters above and any sign of troops below. Mike, knowing they were covering approximately two miles every sixty seconds, moved a finger along the chart at their approximate position and watched for identifiable checkpoints on the ground. John sat erect in his seat, holding the wheel lightly, his right hand ready to hit the throttles. When there was an extra-tall tree, a slight pull on the wheel, almost invisible, would send the Anson zooming an extra twenty-five feet upward. A little forward pressure, just a nudge, would take them back down to fifty feet. John did not look tense, but he did look wide awake. A second's inattention at this speed and altitude would splatter them all over the ground.

"It was great," Ray remembers. "There you were on this peaceful Sunday morning. The Army must have had the day off. Not a soul in sight except friendly guys who would come out of little huts and wave at us.

"It was just like running a sports car; you were very conscious of the speed, you know. It was rather like going on the throughway, with the trees rushing past. It was exhilarating.

"Even at a hundred knots you could see a lot of detail on the ground. I remember two men—I would say they were civil servants because they had white suits on—they looked at us and then one of them dashed inside obviously to telephone.

"And there were other people who were washing their clothes in little pools, looking up, waving."

Twenty minutes after they had turned upriver, they saw the radio tower south of Aba—their first major checkpoint—a little to the left of their path.

John had plotted the course to miss Aba by at least five miles, since the Federal troops were reportedly fighting a successful battle for the city and now occupied most of it.

But on this bright Sunday, there was no sign of fighting in Aba. They were inside the Biafran lines now, and everyone but John could relax a little.

It was time to try raising the tower at Uli airstrip. John felt as though he knew Uli. Every pilot they had talked to had been eager to describe the strip and the hazards of landing there. It was long enough but extremely narrow—actually a mile-long straight section of the main road from Port Harcourt to Kano. When you landed a DC-7 there, you had only eight feet to spare on each side of your main wheels. But the pavement was solid, and rumor had it that the government had laid out this section with deeper foundations and thicker paving for just this purpose, back in the days when England was paying the road bills.

The most difficult thing about landing at Uli was the lighting; flights were usually made at night, with a Nigerian bomber circling overhead trying to catch a plane just landing or taking off. The bright approach lights, off the end of the runway, were usually turned on only for thirty seconds, after a plane had properly identified itself and was actually making its final approach. Setting down a Constellation or a DC-7 with ten tons of food or guns aboard under such conditions required skill, guts and a good bit of luck.

But the crew of the Anson, that Sunday morning, did not have to worry about the darkness. The proper clearance from the tower was the only thing they needed.

Ray got the right frequency on the VHF radio, and John fished his copy of the codes out of his shirt pocket.

The signals required were some of the common phrases you might hear on any aircraft radio, but with a special assigned meaning. "My intercom is out of order" might mean "I'm seeking clearance to land." "Reporting light turbulence" might mean "I'm from Fernando Po."

There was also a set of code letters, different for each day of the week.

John pressed the microphone button and sang out the proper sequence of phrases with the code letters for Sunday.

All three of the crew involuntarily leaned forward, as if it would bring an answering voice nearer. Ray checked and rechecked the receiver frequency.

No answer.

John called again. They could see Owerri off to their left now; they were only fifteen minutes from Uli.

Still no answer.

John had climbed to 1,000 feet to make the radio reception better. Ahead, faintly, he could see the bright green marshland along the Niger River—the eastern boundary of Biafra. Somewhere on this side of it was Uli.

Ray switched to other frequencies, although he knew the first one had been the one always used by planes calling Uli tower. John ran through the code phrases again, feeling a little silly at the meaningless jumble of words. No answer.

Now they were there. John could see what must be the strip ahead. Sharply he banked to the right, staying at least three miles away from the strip; there were antiaircraft guns down there, and there was no use finding out just how strong their lack of welcome was.

They circled for a few minutes, still calling Uli. But fuel was getting down to the halfway point. One last call. Silence. The Anson swung back onto the reverse of the course it had taken out and headed for Fernando Po.

It was a quiet trip back. The weather was still beautiful. No one shot at them. But when they dropped down to the treetops near Aba, for the flight across Federal territory, there wasn't the exhilaration in it that they had felt on the trip out.

They landed back on Fernando Po before 1 P.M. and climbed out over the high piles of food that filled the cabin. John kicked one of the sacks in disgust.

It was four weeks since they had left Bovingdon, and two months since they had first decided to try to help the hungry kids in Biafra. And they still hadn't delivered that first pound of food.

That night John sent in a second letter via an airlift pilot:

URGENT AND CONFIDENTIAL

The Officer Commanding   MERCY MISSIONS
Base-Wing   SANTA ISABEL
                         AIRPORT
Ihiala   FERNANDO PO
                         1st. September 1968

Dear Sir,

I refer to my brief note, hastily sent to you from Sao Tome, last Friday night, 30th August.

As proposed, we attempted to make the first flight to your airfield this morning (1st. September). Unfortunately, bad weather created a difference in our ETA by 90 minutes, and, in addition, we were unable to raise your tower on VHF, using

118.7MCs, and using the codes supplied to us by your authorities at Sao Tome.

Rather than attract hostile attention in the vicinity of your airfield, we aborted North of Aba, and returned to Fernando Po.

We believe, from enquiries we have made, that it is possible that you may be now using different codes from those in our possession; this, no doubt was the reason for the lack of response to our call on 118.7. I am therefore returning herewith, by the hand of Captain Steiner, the code sheets for our two aircraft G-AWMH and G-AWMG. I would ask that you would be good enough to return these to us if the codes have not changed, and these codes are still valid. If, on the other hand, new codes <u>are now in force,</u> we would greatly appreciate your soonest attention to supplying us with new codes—if possible by the return flight to Santa Isabel tonight (Sunday), since we intend, <u>unless otherwise urgently advised,</u> to make our next flight to your airfield tomorrow morning, Monday, Sept. 2nd. ETA 0730-0930 GMT.

We have a cargo of meat, oats, baby food, dried milk, Complan and some supplies for Dr. John Wallace, of the "Save the Children Fund" organization now working in Biafra. We have other supplies of food at present available, together with urgently required medical equipment which will be available to us in the next two to three days.

I am sure that you will appreciate the urgency of our request.

I am, Sir,

Yours faithfully,

John Mitchel Smith, Operations Captain

Mercy Missions.

On Monday morning, September 2, John made one more try to get up-to-date codes for landing at Uli. The Red Cross pilots, who worked for a charter firm named Balair, wanted to help. But they said, they were under orders from the Red Cross not to give Mercy Missions the codes.

"Then to hell with the Red Cross and all the rest," John sputtered. "We'll go in anyway."

He talked to the crew, and they agreed; after coming this far and waiting this long, they didn't feel like sitting still while somebody played politics.

If their motives had at first been mixed, and their loyalties in the war impartial, such was no longer the case. They were ready to do anything to get food moving again into Biafra, and they were now strong partisans of the Biafran cause. The stories told by the Ibo refugees and by airlift pilots who had been harassed by Russian-built Migs had helped do that.

John had noticed that the powdered milk from Church World Service was packed in double-walled heavy paper bags, designed to be dropped from a plane without breaking. The outer bag was loose, so that only the inner one would break when it hit the ground.

"Why don't we pick out a likely refugee camp," John asked the others, "and just drop the stuff in their laps?"

"We can talk to the Thompsons; they'll know where it should go. And the camp won't have to wait for a lorry to bring it over from Uli, using up petrol all the way."

The crew agreed. Sunday's flight had shown them that daylight flights into Biafra were practical. Tony was happy because all four men would be needed—John and Mike to fly and navigate, Ray to push the stuff out the door, and Tony to get it off the piles and back to Ray. And since they would not be landing, they could take their cameras without fear of running afoul of Biafran security men.

The Thompsons shared the enthusiasm and knew just the right spot. It was a leper hospital at Uzuakoli, about nine miles northeast of the Biafran administrative center, Umuahia. It was being used as a refugee camp, but as far as the Chapmans knew, none of the food shipments had been able to get there for weeks. A doctor and a nurse—an old friend of Frances Thompson—were stationed there and could see that the food got fairly distributed.

Uzuakoli would be easy to find, according to the Thompsons. There were a road and a railroad running parallel a couple of miles apart north from Umuahia; where they turned and crossed, you would find the hospital. The sprawl of white, tin-roofed mission buildings would be easy to see from the air, and there was a large yam field which would be a good place to drop the milk.

Frances Thompson was so taken with the plan that she was willing to sacrifice a bed sheet to it. The crew wanted to let Dr. Honey and Sister Gregory know why they were circling over the hospital and forestall any trigger-happy defenders. They also wanted to ask if there were a field suitable for landing anywhere near. Parachutes, they decided, were the way to get the message across.

Mike cut the sheet into four pieces and tied strings to the corners of each piece. The strings of each parachute were tied to a tin box, like a tobacco tin.

While the others sewed and tied, John laboriously copied, in his precise block letters, four copies of the note.

WE ARE FRIENDS AND WE HAVE A LOAD OF DRIED MILK. WE WILL DROP IT NOW ON THE SPOT WHICH LOOKS BEST TO US AND WILL RETURN THIS AFTERNOON WITH ANOTHER LOT.

IF BY THEN YOU HAVE FOUND A SUITABLE LANDING AREA, SIGNAL US BY PUTTING THREE SHEETS OUT ON THE GRASS; IF NOT, PUT OUT TWO SHEETS. IF OUR PRESENCE HERE IS BRINGING DANGER TO US AND YOU DON'T WANT US TO COME BACK, PUT OUT ONE SHEET.

THE LANDING AREA SHOULD BE AT LEAST 75 FEET WIDE AND 1,000 FEET LONG, FLAT, WITH NO WIRES OR TREES AT EITHER END.

When the parachutes and the notes were finished, the crew and the Thompsons put the notes in the tins and then took them upstairs. They stood on the balcony and dropped them, one by one, to see if they worked. They did.

The crew were up at dawn the next day. They lightened the plane, taking out all the cargo that wasn't droppable. They piled the 100-pound sacks of milk—37 of them—as close to the front of the passenger cabin as possible, so the plane wouldn't be tailheavy. They removed the passenger door so the food could be dropped.

While they worked, they had some surprise visitors. A camera team from *Twenty-Four Hours*, the BBC-TV news show, had arrived and wanted to film their preparations and takeoff.

Since *Twenty-Four Hours* had shown an interest in Mercy Missions ever since those first harried days at Bovingdon and had since used some of the film Tony had mailed back from stops along the way, the crew of Mike-Golf were happy to see them. They were glad to hear, too, that the film on Mercy Missions had helped break the unofficial silence about Biafra on British TV, and that news about the civil war was being telecast regularly now.

While the TV camera whirred, Mike-Golf taxied out, got her clearance and roared down the runway toward Biafra again.

The flight at first was a rerun of Sunday's. Tony, seeing the route for the first time, was using up movie film at a spectacular rate. When the coastline appeared, the Anson descended to fifty feet, and this time they hit the mouth of the Kwa Ibo River exactly as planned.

They followed the brown, sluggish stream, not bothering to make the sharper bends but staying generally in the middle of the marshy valley.

It was John who first noticed the troops, hundreds of them, walking through the brush or riding in Land Rovers.

As the Anson roared on toward the line of battle, the concentration of troops became heavier. Ray could see the soldiers look up with a start as they suddenly heard the engines twenty feet overhead. He saw some of them raise their rifles and snap off a shot.

To the left, a huge column of smoke was rising from Aba. The city was on fire, and the crew of the Anson could see lines of refugees on the roads, heading every direction of the compass.

When the Anson crossed the road running directly west from Aba, John banked it around to a course a little east of north, heading for Uzuakoli. Everyone relaxed just a little; they were in friendly territory now, and they could see the railroad—the old-time pilots' "iron compass"—that would lead them straight to the leper colony.

John eased the throttles forward to climb power and

took a minute to flex his elbows and hands as the Anson gained altitude; he could afford to take it easy for the first time since they had seen the coast.

That's when they saw the first rocket.

They thought it was a signal, bursting red a half-mile or so off the starboard wing.

But the next one was closer. Then it was joined by puffs of black smoke—antiaircraft shells. "Hey! They're shooting at us!"

Ray looked down to see not only the antiaircraft batteries, but also infantrymen, everywhere he looked, with their rifles pointed at the Anson and apparently firing away. He could not hear the rifles, of course, and they apparently weren't hitting anything. But they seemed most unfriendly.

Michael was indignant. "What are they shooting at *us* for? Don't they see the red crosses?"

John was trying to remember what he had heard about flak evasion tactics as used in World War II, zigging and zagging the plane while trying to keep an eye out for Uzuakoli.

The flak got thinner and then stopped as they pulled away from Umuahia—and then started up again, thicker than ever. Too late, Ray noticed what seemed to be an oil refinery, ringed with guns, directly below them.

And suddenly they were over the place where the railroad and the highway crossed; there were the tin-roofed buildings and, nearby, the huge yam field with its neat rows of three-foot dirt mounds.

The settlement lay in a broad valley, which narrowed as it rose toward the hills to the north. Overhead, a half-dozen vultures circled lazily.

John flew directly over the mission at 600 feet and then pulled the Anson around in a circle for the parachute drop. Ray fed the chutes out the door one at a time, watching the wind whip them away. He leaned out the open door and saw one of the chutes land right in the yard of the mission residence.

Now John was coming around a second time, losing altitude fast, heading up the valley toward the yam field. Tony lifted one of the sacks of milk off the pile and lugged it back to the door; it weighed two thirds as much as he did. As the brown hillocks of the yam field began flashing past beneath, Ray shoved the sack out the door. Tony brought another, and there was time to get it out before they heard the engines roar and the plane start to climb again.

John, aware of the hills ahead, had determined that when the tops reached a certain point on his windscreen, he would pour on the coal and start climbing. He made a broad circuit of the mission at 200 feet, and then came in from the south again, easing down to twenty-five or thirty feet above the ground. With flaps down, and the engine throttled back to 60 percent power, he was chugging along at maybe eighty miles an hour, trying to make it possible for Ray to get out more bags on each run.

During the letdown, Ray had moved too far from the socket where his intercom was connected and had jerked the plug out. "Can't raise Ray," John said to Mike. "See what's happened." The end of the yam field was coming up fast.

Mike, half-rising against his seat belt and twisting around to see back through the cabin door, got his leg tangled in his own intercom cord and pulled it out. He tried to shout to Ray to get ready.

"What's going on back there?" John yelled.

Ray, standing in the open door, thirty feet above the rushing ground, "suddenly had the feeling something was wrong. Something is very wrong here, I thought. Christ, what's happening?"

What was happening took only a few seconds—
much less than it takes to relate:

The starboard engine had suddenly lost power. The
plane yawed to the right and John's left leg shot out,
holding course with the rudder. The plane sank toward
the ground as John jammed both throttles all the way
forward.

The starboard engine began running again in spurts,
and the plane, almost touching the ground, roared on
straight ahead. John leaned forward, his knuckles
white on the wheel. The plane was just at the edge of
a stall; raise the nose too much and it would stall,
dropping like a stone; raise it too little and it would
soon plow into the rising valley floor.

In a second or so that seemed like an hour, the
Anson began slowly to put space between itself and
the red earth. An inch at a time, it was climbing.

Directly ahead, John saw the tree. Gingerly, because
a plane will stall quicker in a turn, he banked to the
left to go around the tree.

The plane lurched, and the lowered left wing tip hit
one of the dirt mounds. The plane was slammed down
as though on a steel cable and the propellers, first the
left and then the right, sliced through the tops of
mounds, spraying dirt over the windscreen.

Still the Anson stayed in the air, thundering across
the bumps. John was shouting, "Come forward, come
forward!" Out of the corner of his eye, Mike saw
Tony dive headlong onto the pile of milk sacks.

The Anson thudded to the ground, engines roaring,
bounced into the air, hit the ground again and strug-
gled airborne again. The engines, with their props bent
and broken, began to vibrate and shake the whole
plane. John, suddenly aware that she would pound her-
self to pieces before she quit flying, chopped the
throttles. The next time she hit, he pinned her to the

ground with the wheel, and kicked hard right rudder to slew her around in a wild, screeching ground loop.

The nose tore away with a bang and the windscreen shattered. The port engine, its propeller ground to a splintered stub, continued to pop-pop-pop for a moment. Then silence.

As soon as the aircraft came to a stop Mike Draper was out the door and into the bush at the edge of the plowed field. He remembers thinking, "It's going to go up any second."

Then, after the engine stopped kicking over, he began to wonder about John. As he walked back toward the plane, a little guiltily but still wary of an explosion, he saw Tony coming out of the bush on the far side of the field.

John, dazed from a bleeding bump on the head, had got out of his seat and was poking around amongst the sacks of dried milk in the cabin, trying to find his crew. Mike came up to the door and, looking down, saw Ray's dirt-covered body on the ground directly beneath the door. "Ray's dead," he told John.

Just then Ray groaned.

People were starting to gather, coming out of the bush and forming a wide circle around the remnants of Mike-Golf. Some talked excitedly; some just stared. (Later John would learn that a Biafran Army helicopter had crashed nearby just a week before—and that excited citizens had lynched the crew as spies.)

"Is there a doctor here?" John asked the crowd, just as a white man pushed his way through into the circle. "I'm Norman Honey," he said; "I'm the doctor here."

While Ray was carried away, in considerable pain, the other three went to work—at the insistence of the police who had arrived—to camouflage the wreckage.

The crowd helped cut tree branches until the whole thing was covered.

"If a Nigerian plane goes over and sees this plane in this field, he thinks it's an aerodrome," the policeman explained. "Then he bombs us all."

John also went into the cockpit to shut off the ignition and fuel, to avoid any possibility of fire. He found that he and Mike had somehow already done this, in that last second before the final crash. Neither could remember shutting off the fuel cocks, the cross-feed cock, both ignition switches and the master switch. But it had been done.

They surveyed the damage. Mike-Golf's left wing was folded back, intact, parallel to the fuselage. The starboard wing and engine were ripped into chunks and scattered along the path the plane had cut through the yam field. The back part of the fuselage and the tail assembly were twisted upside down, so the tail wheel stuck straight up in the air.

The cockpit and the cabin sat there in one piece. Inside, they found that not one sack of the dried milk had been broken. Mike-Golf might be a total loss, but her cargo—the only one she had had a chance to deliver—had arrived intact.

In the cowling of the right engine they found a small hole—which John thought explained why that engine had suddenly lost power and caused the crash. It looked very much as though Mike-Golf, having overcome all the other obstacles, had been shot down by a rifle in the hands of a Biafran infantryman.

War is not a true adventure. It is a mere ersatz. Where ties are established, where problems are set, where creation is stimulated—there you have adventure. But there is no adventure in heads-or-tails, in betting that the toss will come out of life or death. War is not an adventure. It is a disease. It is like typhus.

—*Flight to Arras*

THE crash had come at 9:05 A.M. By sundown when John Smith sat down to draft a cable to let the people in England know, Ray was safely installed in Queen Elizabeth Hospital in Umuahia, nine miles to the southeast.

Tony had bruises that wouldn't permit him to sit down for three days yet, but Mike didn't have a scratch.

John's head cut had been stitched shut (without benefit of anesthetic, which was in short supply) in the operating room of the Queen Elizabeth Hospital that afternoon. While the surgeon was working, John was dimly aware of the fact that doctors were removing bullets from wounded soldiers on the other two operating tables in the same room. The front was just a little over twenty miles away.

The cablegram, which would have to be taken out by one of the Red Cross pilots and sent from Fernando Po, was addressed to the *Twenty-Four Hours* program of the BBC. John and the crew had left all their cash on the island, and the BBC was the only organization they knew that might accept a collect cable.

This was the text:

GOING TO HAVE SPOIL STORY. FAILED THROUGH
PARTIAL FAILURE OF STARBOARD ENGINE AT LOW
HEIGHT. ALREADY WE HAVE SEEN ENOUGH TO KNOW
THAT THIS JOB IS WORTHWHILE, AND I WOULD ASK
IF YOU COULD MAKE AN APPEAL FOR US FOR CASH,
SO WE CAN FINALIZE PURCHASE OF OTHER AIRCRAFT
AND GET ON WITH IT. CREW SAFE WITH MINOR
THINGS EXCEPT ROBERTS, WHO IS IN HOSPITAL
WITH PELVIS PROBLEM, BUT EXPECTS TO RETURN
IN THREE DAYS TO FERNANDO PO.

JOHN M. SMITH

MERCY MISSIONS

It was true that Ray had a problem; standing in the
door of the plane when it hit, he had been thrown
straight down to the ground, breaking his pelvis. But
the prediction that Ray—or any of the Mercy Missions
crew—would be out of Biafra in three days turned out
to be wildly optimistic.

A hint of the trouble ahead was in a letter written
by Dr. Wallace, the energetic young man from the
Save the Children Fund whom John had tried to help
on Fernando Po. Wallace wrote his wife the day after
the crash:

. . . At Uzuakoli we found John Smith with a
small scalp laceration, Michael Draper and Anthony
Stancomb having lunch with Dr. Honey, who is
responsible for them while the Biafran authorities
inquire into their credentials.

We came into Umuahia to see how Roberts was.
He is in a side ward off Slessor Ward, with a very
competent American nursing sister in charge and a
security guard at the door.

Roberts is still in quite a bit of pain from a

fractured pelvis sustained when he was thrown out of the open door as the plane came in. He is under the professor's care. He had a blood transfusion, but is not fit to be moved yet.

The attitude here apparently is one of suspicion mixed with admiration that anyone could have been so foolhardy, and naturally he and they will have to be cleared with the foreign ministry here and presumably with the Spanish on Fernando Po before they can go.

Except for the pain, Ray was in great shape. His doctor had been chief professor of surgery at the University of Ibadan, the best university in Africa, before the war. Like a high percentage of the faculty there, he was an Ibo and had chosen to come back to join Biafra's fight for independence.

The hospital was run along English lines, and many of the nurses were trained in England. The care was efficient and pleasant.

Queen Elizabeth Hospital was a sprawling series of buildings, concrete block with wide overhanging tin roofs. Each ward was a building by itself. Usually every bed was full, but when the fighting got more intense at Aba, there would also be a patient on a mat between each bed, and others in rows along the verandas surrounding each building. Somehow the staff managed not only to care for all these patients, but also to show that they were concerned about each one.

The heat was bad, but an orderly often would bring in a large fan on a floor stand. It was taken away only when there was a large influx of wounded from the Aba front.

Ray remembered nothing at all about the crash. "I remember being in a lot of pain," he told Dr. Wallace. "And being carried. And knowing that something had happened to me. And I think brandy being forced in between my teeth.

"And I remember old Tony waving his movie camera at me."

Even a tiny country fighting for its life against great odds has red tape. Maybe even more of it than normal.

The Mercy Missions crew began to see this when an immigration official arrived on the crowded yam field, soon after the crash, and asked them for their passports and visas.

But they hadn't expected to land, they explained, and all but John had left their passports on the island. What's more, only John and Ray had bothered to get visas, since they were the only two—way back then in London—who had planned to go into Biafra. They had no visas for Fernando Po either, they explained in answer to his question, because they were considered as aircrew in transit.

They had agreed to ask the Red Cross pilots to bring the passports in on the first available plane. The immigration man hadn't said much, except that they were in Dr. Honey's custody and shouldn't leave the refugee camp. His tone of voice indicated that he would be back.

It soon became evident to John that they were not going to be able just to get on a plane and fly out.

It was a week before John's cablegram on its roundabout route reached England. But the Twenty-Four Hours camera team on Fernando Po knew there was trouble when the Anson failed to return. They sent their film by air to London.

By coincidence, Peter Cadogan was in the BBC studio when the film was developed. "Hello!" the film editor exclaimed as he ran the film for the first time; "Your boys didn't come back from their ride!"

Maxine Roberts was in the living room–dining room of the Roberts' second-floor flat in Watford, that evening, "just sitting there looking at the tele," she recalls. "Then the news came on." There was film of the loading of the Anson the previous Tuesday, and she saw Ray turn and grin as he ducked into the cabin. The takeoff was shown, and then the commentator added, "The crew have not returned from that flight; it must be presumed that they encountered trouble and may have crashed in Nigeria."

Carol Libby, Mike's girl, didn't know until she went to work at the bank on Saturday morning. One of the other clerks thrust a paper in front of her and asked, "Have you seen this?" The headline read: FOUR BRITONS SHOT DOWN.

Less than a mile away, Sue had been living out of a suitcase for nearly a month, waiting for word that she should join John on Fernando Po. When she heard that the Anson was missing she began checking airline flights to the island, although she had no way of knowing whether John was alive or not. She planned to leave in a week. But on the fifth day, she received a cablegram that had been forwarded by the Foreign Office.

It said, DO NOT COME YET. It was signed, JOHN. The fact that John Smith never sent it is just one of the mysteries that haunted the crew in the next few weeks.

At Uzuakoli, the rest of the crew were getting used to conditions quite different from those Ray enjoyed in the hospital.

Their living quarters were quite comfortable; Dr. Honey had room for Tony and John, and Sister Gregory's house had an extra room for Mike. They

were accepted as part of the mission family. But the
scene around the mission was something their imagina-
tions had not prepared them for.

"I was walking along the road just outside the camp
the second day," John recalls, "and I saw these gray
logs lined up along the side.

"Then I saw that they weren't logs, they were
bodies, covered with ash. Mostly they were children."

Sleeping in the open or in makeshift shelters around
the hospital compound, the crew saw what seemed to
be several thousand people—mostly children, women
and old men. Norman Honey said there were probably
four million refugees in Biafra right now. Most of
them lived in the woods or in villages where they were
unwelcome and got little help; only 700,000 were in
camps such as this one, run by various church and
charity organizations under the Biafran Red Cross.

Many of the adults fit the picture of the natives in
an old geography textbook, wearing nothing but a
rag around the middle. But John noticed that the
women covered their breasts when the doctor, the crew
or other visitors came by. "They aren't naked because
it's tribal custom," Dr. Honey explained. "It's just that
the clothes they had are lost or worn out; what you
see on them is literally all they own."

There had been no food shipment to the Uzuakoli
camp for six weeks, but on the morning after the crash
of the Anson people began arriving by the hundreds
to get some of the powdered milk. There were families
on the move, the crew learned, perpetually in quest of
food. When there was word of a shipment, they'd
begin making their way there.

The children would stand on one side of the compound, often more than a thousand of them. On the
other side would be an equal number of women, near
them, a handful of old men. The adults waited quietly,

but the children might be singing one of the odd new "hymns" that combined patriotism and religion for Biafrans, like:

> We are Biafrans
> Fighting for our land.
> In Jesus' holy name
> We shall conquer yet.

Or, to the tune of another old hymn, they might be singing,

> Praise him, praise him,
> Ojukwu our leader will conquer . . .

The milk was given out, dry, in little bags for those who preferred it that way. For the others it was mixed with water and ladled from a bucket into the containers the youngsters eagerly held out.

The crew soon learned to recognize kwashiorkor, the disease of malnutrition that produces swollen bellies, yellow-orange hair, and saucerlike eyes with an apathetic stare. "If the hair has already turned color," Norman Honey explained, "it's probably too late; there isn't much chance of recovery."

And, almost against their will, they learned the terrible chemistry of hunger. They learned because it was happening to the people who showed up in increasing numbers each dawn at the camp.

The first few days without food, they learned, there are cramps and bloating as the stomach shrinks in size. During this stage children will cry a great deal and will eat anything—grass, rags, twigs and even dirt— to stop the hunger pangs.

In a few days the child is too weak to do much but whimper. Now he is suffering from nausea, resulting from the fact that his body is burning up all its stored fat. Without adequate carbohydrates to balance the fat, he is in the same physical situation as a diabetic on an improperly balanced diet; he may actually go into diabetic coma.

The next stage is recognizable from the lethargy that overtakes the youngster; he sleeps much of the time as nature tries to ease his dying. Meanwhile, since his body proteins are depleted, the ability of his body to dispose of water is affected. His arms and legs may become swollen with water to the point where they split the skin like sausages. Irreversible damage to his liver and kidneys is taking place, and this affects his ability to fight infection and disease.

If a child at this stage is put on an adequate, balanced diet, he still will probably suffer the rest of his life from the damage to vital organs.

These were the children the crew had come to help. And even if this wasn't what they had hoped to be doing, they pitched in, working long days, helping around the compound. There were things to repair, and children to be played with, food to be distributed, and errands to run. At the end of the first week a lorry arrived with food from the Norchurchaid flight, the first such load in six weeks. John and the crew unloaded it and helped mix the powdered protein with grated yams to make a yellow, powdery gruel called garri. It tasted a little like cornmeal, and a few days of it made a visible difference in the health of a child.

Although their main concern was the children, the crew couldn't help hearing the boom of guns on the Aba front. They knew that even the most optimistic of the missionaries were predicting that Biafra couldn't last more than another month. And they worried about getting Ray out.

The message from the foreign ministry in Umuahia

had been "just a few more days, while we check your papers." It was the same a few days later, and again a few days after that.

They tried venturing outside the compound but found that every road had frequent checkpoints; it was impossible to go more than a mile in any direction without being stopped. And without a pass, you could not go on.

Even John, who had been given the okay to leave the area around the mission, had trouble moving about. But he had noticed that the World Council of Churches workers were never stopped. He managed to loosen a blue-and-white paper sticker bearing the World Council name and its symbol, a ship, from the box to which it was glued. He carefully slit a button-hole in the tattered paper and hung it from the button on the left pocket of his shirt.

From then on he could move more freely, given entrée by his "official" World Council of Churches identification badge.

The crew thoroughly enjoyed the company of Nor-man Honey and his nurse, Sister Gregory, who by now they were calling Greg. And the two medical workers obviously appreciated having the others around for the rare moments of relaxation and at meals.

The table talk often dwelt on "great meals I have eaten," with imagination assisting memory to bring forth visions of succulent roast beef, thick soups, fresh salads and exotic desserts. All this was carried on over plates whose main contents were yams—which, no matter how imaginatively they are cooked, still taste like yams.

Occasionally in the market they could get an egg or two, and bananas and oranges. But the only meat was a tin or two brought in by a visitor now and then.

The talk often turned to the three scrawny chickens that Greg kept as pets. They had long since stopped laying eggs, since the local diet wasn't good enough even to keep chickens happy. But Greg refused to consider any other use the chickens might have.

"It'll take another war," she would snap, "to get these chickens away from me!"

She would get her revenge for the teasing, though, when introducing John or Mike to one of the frequent visitors who came through. "This is just a little English pilot," she would say, "who fell into my back garden one morning."

In the middle of their second week at Uzuakoli, the crew had a visitor. He turned out to be Superintendent Okokomkwo of the special security police. Though always polite, he had many questions, and he obviously was not satisfied that the crew were telling him the whole truth.

"Mr. Cadogan told us to expect you on the seventeenth or eighteenth of August," he said. "We know you arrived on Fernando Po around then. Why did you wait so long to come to Biafra?"

John spread his hands. "The Red Cross refused to give us food to fly in, and we had to make arrangements to have it flown over from São Tomé."

The superintendent smiled. "Come now, gentlemen. Surely the Red Cross would not refuse assistance from people who offered to help. Actually, now, what was the real reason for spending so much time on the island?"

Tony remembers thinking that the whole thing was like Camus's *The Plague*. "It was no surprise that they thought we were spies. Everyone in Biafra seemed to be suspicious of everyone else. They were denouncing one another with great gusto."

The suspicion was not difficult to understand. This was a civil war, with tribe set against tribe and even brother against brother. There had been trickery, and spies, and poisonings; in the background of the war was a coup in which officers had killed brother officers, including their own tribesmen. And the major power now aligned against the Biafrans was the country from which the Mercy Missions crew came.

It was not difficult to understand. But it was not easy to take, and understanding it made the danger no less real.

Dr. Honey's house, which had been searched before by Biafran troops, was searched three times while the crew was there. And a group of villagers accused Sister Gregory of being a spy.

The Britishers in the compound were only too well aware that some important groups in Biafra would have liked to put an Englishman on trial. It would be a chance for a public show of feelings toward the British foreign policy and would be another boost to Biafran patriotism.

But each day came, and with it no arrests. Just the questions. Superintendent Okokomkwo visited Ray in the hospital. "We found a Nigerian flag in your aircraft. How did it get there?"

"How stupid do you think we are?" Ray asked. "If we were spies, do you think we'd be dumb enough to bring along a Nigerian flag? I don't know where you got your flag, but it wasn't in our Anson."

On another visit the superintendent produced a carbon copy of a cable Ray had received in Fernando Po three weeks earlier. It was from an editor in London, accepting Ray's proposal to send some pictures from Biafra, and ending with a line the editor had mistakenly intended to be helpful: "We have a good man in Lagos whom you may want to contact."

"Just what are you contacting people in Lagos about?" the policeman wanted to know.

There was also a question about the cameras Ray and Tony had brought along. They had denied being journalists—and as a matter of fact, their function on the crew was not as journalists. But Ray's passport, when it finally arrived from Fernando Po, said "Photographer" in the space marked "Occupation."

For several days, the questioning centered on the crew's arrival at São Tomé.

"Why did you choose that particular date?" the officer wanted to know. "Why did you arrive at that time in the afternoon and then leave the next day? What made you choose the sixteenth of August for your arrival at the island?"

The men thought of all the variables that had affected their schedule—the rain at Jersey and the cracked wheel at Bilbao. The truculent tower operator at Dakar. The fouled-up boost control on the port engine. The decision to come direct from Abidjan rather than via Accra.

But the officer wasn't convinced. Englishmen didn't operate in such haphazard fashion. They planned carefully and operated according to the plan they had made.

"Come, come, gentlemen," he said, slapping his swagger stick against his palm. "What was the real reason you had to get to São Tomé on the evening of August sixteenth?"

It wasn't until weeks later that John learned why there was so much interest in the date. "Didn't you know," he was asked, "that on that night in São Tomé there was a meeting of representatives of all the major arms dealers in the world talking about getting guns into Biafra? The Army thinks you must have had a special interest in guns, rather than food, or you wouldn't have worked so hard to arrive just on that day!"

While the suspicion and pressure from the Biafran officials were growing, the little group at Uzuakoli was becoming more and more aware of the approaching Nigerian Army.

"We were sitting on the veranda having coffee at eleven o'clock in the morning," Mike remembers. "And we heard these jets. I got up to go have a good look, and when I got to the door I realized that this was a bit nearer than the others had been.

"And as I stood in the doorway there I saw him turn and come in straight for the house and it looked as though he was just going to shoot the hell out of the house.

"And Greg was saying, 'Hide here' and 'into the bedroom,' and 'under the sofa,' and all this sort of thing. Absolute flap, and all she was doing was standing in the middle of the room, turning around.

"And suddenly—it's quite a graphic memory— there were six rockets let go from underneath the wings. I threw myself down. And they exploded just behind the house—just a boom, boom, boom, boom, boom, boom. In rapid succession.

"Didn't kill anybody. But one rocket landed in the market, injuring a lot of women and children. Norman went down immediately and amputated this one man's leg. . . ."

Since Uzuakoli was on the main road between Umuahia and the nearest fighting, the grapevine was active and, sometimes, even accurate. The Nigerian division that had taken Onitsha was now pushing steadily toward the airstrip. They were within twenty miles on two sides.

Aba, the major city on the south perimeter, had fallen and was now the center of a large half-circle cut deeply into the Biafran border. Owerri, to the south-east, was under heavy attack. In the north, Nigerian divisions were advancing toward one another from Onitsha and Enugu, along the main road between those towns. If they met, it would isolate the whole northern section, one-fourth of Biafra's territory.

The fact that Biafra had lasted this long was a miracle, of course. The war had ground on for fourteen months, and during all that time Nigeria was receiving arms and ammunition from both Great Britain and Russia. Nigeria had six times the population from which to draw her soldiers. It had Lagos, one of the best seaports in Africa, and Port Harcourt, recaptured from Biafra months before. It had the rich oil fields of the eastern region—originally Biafra's hope for self-sufficiency—and could thus count on support and cash from the big oil companies. It had friendly neighbors on three sides and the ocean on the fourth.

The Nigerians' most effective weapon, a Biafran officer told the Mercy Missions crew, was the armored vehicle. Great Britain was sending its newest and fastest: the Saladdin, the Saracen and the Ferret. British 105-mm howitzers and 155-mm artillery were bought through Italy. They used Russian-made rockets, a lot of them, and British-made rifles, the most modern kind.

The pilots of the Russian-built Mig 17 fighters and Ilyushin twin-jet bombers came from Egypt and from East Germany, he said. Russians maintained the aircraft and kept them armed. And the British Army furnished officers as advisers for most headquarters outfits down to the brigade level.

Biafra, on the other hand, had to deal for her arms on the world market—an expensive and sometimes shady proposition. (French arms did not begin to arrive until two months later, near the end of 1968.) Her only "port" was the inadequate airstrip at Uli, which she dared use only at night. She was not recognized as a country by any of the major powers of the world; in fact, only four African nations had recognized the government. There was no outside source of money to replace the oil wells she had lost. She was completely surrounded, forced to maintain her border by arms.

The Biafran troops that marched past the leper colony often had no shoes. Many still wore the ragged clothes they had on when they were drafted. Some of them, on their way to the battle around Ake Eze, told the crew they had had only two weeks of training.

And some of them were going to war without guns. There were just not enough to go around. But the soldiers seemed confident. "The men who do have guns will soon capture enough for the rest of us," one man said.

One reason why the Biafrans hadn't been licked was obvious from their manner as they marched past. They were singing songs about victory for Biafra. They shouted slogans deriding the Nigerians. They were smiling. They showed a confidence that wasn't very logical, but was very real.

Another reason Biafra was still alive was that the alternative was unthinkable. From Lieutenant Colonel Ojukwu, the chief of state, down to the poorest refugee shuffling from one feeding center to another, they all believed that to surrender to the Nigerians meant sure death.

Politicians and the world press could argue the point all they wanted; they could believe in genocide or ridicule it. The fact was that the Biafrans believed it and had seen enough evidence to go on believing it. They were a people struggling not just for a new nation, but for their own lives and the lives of all their tribesmen. The fanatic determination that grows from such a belief had helped keep the Nigerians at bay for months.

Another secret weapon was brains. The majority of the doctors, chemists, dentists, biologists, and other scientists and professional men in the country had been Ibos. A few stayed in their posts in Nigeria, even after the massacres and the secession, but most had come back to the tribal region to fight with Biafra.

Now these men were applying the most modern techniques of their professions to primitive tools for a primitive war. A former professor of physics from the University of Nigeria, trained in England and America, headed a science group known as the Research and Production Directorate. Among other things, the group had learned how to build portable oil refineries, producing gasoline with the heat from a wood fire. They had made mortars from oil-drilling equipment. With available materials they were producing matches, soap, rocket launchers and gin.

But now, in mid-September of 1968, the Nigerian might and power was beginning to tell. The Army was no longer training men for the kind of war in which you defend a front; even the strategists at the top agreed that in a month Biafra as a physical reality would probably be gone.

Instead, the Army was concentrating on training its best men for what it called Phase Two: guerrilla warfare in the hills. They knew what it had taken the Americans so long to learn in Vietnam: that a small, light, hit-and-run army can stand off a force ten times its size. They were prepared to take to the bush with their homemade armaments, their families and their dreams of a place called Biafra.

The Biafrans were counting heavily on hired professional soldiers to carry on this training, since there were so few experienced Biafran officers. Led by a South African nicknamed Mad Major Williams, they included veterans of the Congo revolution like Marc Goossens and Marc Boucher; Arman Anarelli, a former OAS terrorist, and the famous Colonel Steiner.

In a few months Goossens would be killed in battle and the rest would be expelled for displeasing Lieutenant Colonel Ojukwu. But in September the Mercy Missions crew, undergoing round after round of suspicious questions by the security police, were amused to hear Biafra Radio always refer to the white mercenaries as "our Christian brothers who have come to help."

One night Mike was listening to Radio Nigeria, the Federal station, when he got a rude shock. The commentator read off the names of the four Mercy Missions crewmen and denounced them as mercenaries! "When the Federal forces capture Umuahia," the newsman said, "these soldiers of fortune will be the first to be chopped up by the victorious troops."

Most of the Europeans still in the area had escape plans of one kind or another. One group agreed, if they were surrounded, to build a little Red Cross stockade and huddle together inside, welcoming the Federal troops as "liberators."

But the Mercy Missions crew knew they could not run—not as long as Ray was penned up in the hospital.

Actually, Ray wasn't any too safe where he was.

Umuahia was getting daily visits, promptly at 10:30 A.M., from the Nigerian bombers, whose loads seemed to fall perilously close to the hospital where Ray was. There was a railroad siding and a fuel storage depot right alongside the hospital, and these seemed to be the main targets—although the experience of other towns showed that the Egyptian pilots flying the Russian Ilyushin bombers had no objection to bombing hospitals that stood off all alone, with red crosses painted all over their roofs.

"They asked me if I wanted to get under the bed when the planes came over," Ray says, "but I couldn't be bothered.

"Even with the cast, I could have done it if I'd had to. In fact, I was thinking out ways, if I really saw that ceiling moving, to get under the bed or pull it over on me."

The crew by now had permission to go into Umuahia and were making the trip to camp on the doorstep of the Foreign Minister every time they could find a vehicle and some gasoline.

Umuahia was Biafra's "administrative center"—a euphemism adopted by the press because the capital, Enugu, had been captured months before. But all official documents continued to be stamped "Enugu." The *Daily Sun*, printed on blue-lined writing paper, carried the legend "Printed at Enugu, Biafra." Radio Enugu continued to broadcast official Biafran information—but from a point seventy miles south of the city for which it was named.

Enugu, according to the reports, was now a ghost town. But Umuahia (pronounced "You-MY-uh") was booming. Before the war it was a market town of 35,000 people; now it had at least 100,000 inhabitants.

The scars of war were obvious all over town. Hundreds of houses and shops had been bombed. The railroad station was a shell, although the trains still ran. A church near the hospital was camouflaged with palm branches, because of the bomber pilots' penchant for hitting churches.

People rose early; Ray could hear the recruits from the training camps double-timing down the hill past the hospital, singing war songs, at 6 A.M.

The shops (like the houses, made of cement or mud block with tin roofs) opened for business at 8 A.M. When they had anything to sell, that is. The Ibos had been Nigeria's traders, and they knew the value of a scarce item. Salt was going for $7 a cup, and cigarettes for $10 a pack. A tailored cotton dress would bring $40, and a pair of shoes $25.

Civil servants moved in crowds through the market on their way to work, walking or riding bicycles to save gasoline. Women came in from nearby villages with bundles of wood or bananas on their heads. A few had eggs, at seventy cents apiece.

But by ten o'clock the market place was empty, and the shops were shuttered. Soon the Nigerian bombers would be back, and everyone knew how the pilots liked to go for crowds.

The Foreign Office was a low, tin-roofed building like all the rest. To get in, you had to convince a suspicious young sergeant who carried a submachine gun, and then state your case to an even younger lieutenant who sat behind a wooden desk. Even when you had been there many times before you had to go through the whole scene.

Usually the top men in the office were too busy to see John and Tony. If one of them did agree to talk, he had no encouragement to offer. Where once it had been, "We haven't quite finished with your passports," now it was, "These passports of yours are obviously forged."

One accusation by the Biafrans actually was good news to the crew. "The British government is making inquiries about you," they were told. "We know that a huge government like Her Majesty's would not concern itself with so small a matter unless you men were indeed on some special mission."

Still, they were not arrested. The Biafrans did not

want to let them go, or even wander around inside the country, but they obviously were not yet ready to put them in jail either. They merely acted increasingly suspicious and unfriendly.

The crew went back to Uzuakoli that night discouraged as usual; on the way they heard the rumble of big guns somewhere far away. But they knew the British government was concerned, and that left them feeling a little less alone.

As a matter of fact, there were several people trying to find out why the Mercy Missions crew was still in Biafra.

S. A. Dunn, the British consul on Fernando Po, sent a letter with the airlift, urging the crew to "come out as soon as you can, by whatever route is open to you. . . .

"The Federals are supposed to be pushing closer all the time, and I expect you will know more about this than we do, but please do not discount the possibility of your being mistaken for mercenaries in the event of being over-run. I am not sure, either, just how long it will be possible for any planes to land in Biafra. . . ."

He had heard reports that Ray was in the hospital, he said, but did not know how seriously he was hurt. London was undoubtedly doing something to get action, he added, but "I am not aware of how much."

The business in London was tricky. The Foreign Office there did not recognize Biafra and officially could not admit that it existed. However, there were channels for communication with Biafra House, the unofficial embassy.

Peter Cadogan was also making daily calls at Biafra House and was reporting regularly to Sue, Carol and Maxine, the women the crew had left behind.

And in Uzuakoli, the crew received a most welcome letter from Charles Bailiff. Charles, the man John had turned down for a ride from São Tomé because he "looked like a junkie," and who had been responsible for getting cargo for them at Fernando Po, was now working at getting them out of Biafra.

The letter is worth rereading, because it shows the problems Bailiff was up against:

Dear John, Tony, Mike and Ray:

Well, what can I say? I'm in the dark as much as everyone else as to what really happened and why you are still in there. I have been unable to elicit any information thereon, either, despite the fact that we have sent several letters in.

I have tried for several days to get Biafran clearance to go in, having been turned back at the airport by the Red Cross when I tried to board one of their planes (the Balair) several nights ago. After days of silence Mr. Dunn and I decided it would be better to send in the passports. Also, I was dismayed that Dr. Lindt told the BBC before they left that he would not allow your evacuation on a Red Cross plane unless Lagos as well as Biafra agreed. Therefore I am trusting that you will leave via a São Tomé plane as soon as you are able. I am sure that the pro-Biafra lobby in Britain's parliament will be strengthened tomorrow when the BBC releases the news tomorrow that you aren't allowed to leave on a Red Cross plane without Lagos' permission!!

Then Bailiff added a note obviously directed at any Biafran immigration official who would read it:

Similarly, I indicated to the BBC in a filmed interview (to be shown tomorrow) last Friday just before they left for London that I was certain that by now the government of the Republic of Biafra had easily assured itself of your good intentions toward it, simply by verifying with Biafra House in London and/or the Biafra delegation with whom we talked in São Tomé, and who gave you the code a few weeks ago.

I know—at least I confidently reassure myself— that the Christian Ibos of Biafra whom I have known so well will extend you every cooperative effort out of gratitude for what you tried to do. Certainly you have won the respect of men of good will everywhere.

He added that he had sent a cablegram to Dr. Ibiam, one of the six vice-presidents of the World Council of Churches, who was a pro-Biafra Ibo and a close associate of Ojukwu.

Another postscript, for John, said that "your wife is not here yet but is expected."

Bailiff's determination to help—even if it meant coming into Biafra—impressed the crew. They knew that he hated flying.

He wrote again a few days later to say that a representative from the World Council of Churches office had been on Fernando Po to negotiate with the Red Cross the question of releasing the relief supplies originally made available by the WCC. The representative, Charles wrote, had "regretted he didn't get to meet you but agreed to talk with Dr. Francis Ibiam on your behalf."

And he wrote that "we are all concerned, as the Federals say here they consider you mercenaries as a result of your trip to São Tomé. Not to alarm you but please try to leave via São or Gabon plane if ICRC won't let you."

13

It may be glorious to die for the expansion of territory, but modern warfare . . . is no longer war, it is a kind of bloody surgery. Each side settles down behind a concrete wall and finds nothing better to do than send forth, night after night, squadrons of planes. . . . Such a war is won by him who rots last—but in the end both rot together.

—*Wind, Sand and Stars*

ON Sunday, September 15, a Biafran minister visited the chapel at Uzuakoli and delivered a sermon that was a blistering attack on Britain, the British people and all things that could be labeled British.

It was the start of a strange and unforgettable week, in which the crew grew into an increasingly familiar routine while at the same time the pressure and the tension continued to grow.

The first Norchurchaid relief plane that night came over Uzuakoli en route to the Uturu airstrip at 6:40, five minutes before sunset. It was the earliest Mike had ever seen the airlift operating; apparently the little airstrip was going to be handling a steady stream of flights until dawn.

You could always tell when the planes were coming because five minutes earlier in their flight (thirty miles to the west) they were still in Nigerian-held territory; you could hear the faint boom-boom-boom of the anti-aircraft guns, and then the roar of the big Douglas' four engines, rising and falling in pitch as they dove, zoomed and zigzagged to keep from getting hit. You couldn't see the flashes from the exploding flak. You just heard the guns and the straining engines, and in a few minutes the big plane came whistling overhead, its engines already throttled back and flaps partway down for the descent from 18,000 feet.

On Monday, the sixteenth, John and Tony had an appointment with the Foriegn Secretary. They hitched a ride to Umuahia, hoping that this would be the day they would get their clearance to leave Biafra.

But the police wanted to ask some questions first and intercepted them; by the time they had finished, the time for the appointment had passed, and the Foreign Secretary was no longer available.

That evening they heard that Owerri had fallen. The major town on the southeastern border, it was less than twenty-five miles from the Uli airstrip. Nigerian troops were now in a position to move south from Onitsha and north from Owerri to cut off the main road connecting the two airstrips with all of eastern Biafra—including Umuahia and Uzuakoli.

That night Mike, ever the plane-spotter, made a note of the first Lockheed Super-Constellation he'd seen flying the airlift. It came over just at sunset, bound for Uturu. And on the BBC world news, Mike and Tony heard the announcement that a UNICEF helicopter had crashed in Federal territory.

On Tuesday, the seventeenth, John and Tony again made the ten-mile trip into Umuahia, and this time they got to see the Foreign Secretary. He was very polite, but he regretted that he was unable to grant permission either to move about freely or to leave Biafra just yet. There were too many unanswered questions about their credentials, and about their original intentions in coming.

Susan Garth, the wealthy English woman who had been raising money on both sides of the Atlantic for Biafran children, arrived that day in Umuahia. She announced that she was going to "kidnap Harold Wilson and drag him down to Biafra by the nape of the neck" to see what British guns were doing to the children. A striking character full of a mixture of enthusiasm and indignation, she promised to have the hunger situation cleared up within weeks. She had made a brief tour of feeding centers roaring down the road in a Land Rover.

(Later, she would be in trouble with the law both in London and New York over her handling of funds. She was not embezzling the money; she was a wealthy woman who had put much of her own capital into the project. It was just that she seemed unable to keep track of the cash in compliance with local law, or to set up procedures for funneling it in the best way to the groups who needed it most.)

That was also the evening when the crew learned that Nick Taaffe had finally turned up in Fernando Po. But elation quickly turned to discouragement when they got the rest of the message: Nick had arrived without his airplane. Mike-Hotel and John Desborough, the copilot, were still back in Port Étienne.

John sent out, by the same messenger, a rather abrupt note to Nick and a letter to Mr. S. A. Dunn, the British consul on Fernando Po, reporting the latest failure in his efforts to get the crew released.

They said good-bye that night to Clyne Shepherd, a World Council relief supervisor who had shown concern over their problems and had helped them in their efforts to get out. Now, worn out from months of this kind of tension, he was going on leave and might not be back. For the crew, it was a lonely leave-taking.

That night came one of several arguments amongst the crew. The tension, the incessant muggy heat and the steady diet of yams were driving them all up the wall. And they were beginning to take it out on each other.

Why had Tony and Ray insisted on bringing their cameras, John wanted to know. That was the basis of all the trouble from the Biafrans.

Why was John spending so much time in Umuahia to so little effect, Mike wanted to know. Was he working on some deal that would put him in good with the Biafrans, maybe a flying deal, while the rest of them worked and worried?

Why had John flown so low over the yam field? Why had Tony hidden his cameras after the crash instead of giving them to the police right away?

The arguments were hot, but they never lasted long. And the hostility didn't last long either; even as they battled they knew what they were saying was based more on frustration than on facts.

They had been in Biafra two weeks now, and it was becoming more and more plain that they were in real trouble. The Biafrans might stop playing cat-and-mouse and clap them in jail any moment; the Federals might arrive any day.

But the hardest thing to take was what they felt to be the complete failure of their mission. As long as the other Anson was waiting in the wings, they could dream of someday resuming the low-level daylight flights. This would show Peter Cadogan, their families and the British press that the original idea had been a good one.

But Nick's arrival without his airplane made them wonder whether there ever would be another Mercy Missions flight.

On Wednesday, September 18, John, Mike and Tony decided to go into town to see the lady everyone was describing as "this madwoman, Susan Garth." A traveler reported that she had confronted the mighty Ojukwu, a man who put great value on the dignity of his office, shaking her finger in his face and calling him "a naughty boy." She had thumped the desk of the Foreign Secretary and demanded that he "stop playing war with the lives of children."

The Biafran chiefs, who later in the month would expel the famed mercenary Colonel Steiner for failing to show proper respect, reportedly were struck dumb by the English woman's attack.

John had borrowed a car, which broke down after lurching only a couple of miles toward Umuahia. The road hadn't been repaired in months, except in a few spots where bomb craters had been filled in. In places where a tree had fallen, a new set of tire tracks had been made out around it, usually remaining in use even after the original obstacle rotted away.

John thought the car's troubles were caused by the petrol, which he described as "no more than colored water," and insisted the car could be restarted by pushing. Despite occasional surges of life from the engine, they pushed it much of the way to Umuahia.

They had picked up a hitchhiker, a young Army private on his way back to Umuahia, thinking that his presence in the left-front seat would help them through the six or eight roadblocks they faced.

Now, every time the engine stopped, he would jump out and walk around the car, thumping and kicking vigorously its various parts. What scared the Englishmen, who retreated to the side of the road at least ten yards away every time this happened, was that the butt of his submachine gun, slung over his shoulder, kept banging against the car. They expected it to go off any moment.

They arrived in Umuahia in late afternoon to find that the indomitable Miss Garth had left. But they had another errand to perform: turning in Tony's and Ray's cameras to Superintendent Okokomkwo. The police obviously knew about the cameras and kept asking questions about them, but they had never demanded possession of them. Now, at the insistence of John and Mike, the cameras were being handed over. For Tony, who had nearly a thousand dollars tied up in equipment, it seemed an expensive way to show good faith.

Late that night, after a wearing trip back to Uzuakoli, the crew were about to go to bed when they heard a truck pull into the compound.

It was Charles Bailiff, grinning weakly at the resulting tumultuous welcome, but looking a little pale.

"Never again," he told Mike. "I'll never get in an airplane again."

The trip was one he could describe only as "terrible, terrible."

There were no seats in the plane, he said, and no seat belts. He had been sitting on a wooden box when the pilot suddenly tilted the plane right up on one wing. The wings were vertical, he said, and he could see flashes out the windows on both sides—above them and below them—from the flak exploding all around the plane.

Then the pilot had wrenched the plane around the other way, tilting up on the other wing. He dived and then climbed. Boxes were sliding around inside the plane, and Charles was flopping loose amongst them.

The Mercy Missions crew showed the usual amount of sympathy bestowed by aircrew upon airsick passengers; they rolled on the floor laughing. They asked Charles if he had forgotten the pillbox he always carried. With a grin he pulled out his little box with, Mike says, "every different color pill you could think of, including headache pills, cold pills and airsick pills."

Charles had come to find out why the Biafrans were still holding them here and to confer with Dr. Middelkoop, who had been evacuated from the bush hospital where he and his family had served for years; it was now in Nigerian hands. Charles and Dr. Middelkoop, serving as World Council representatives in Biafra, intended to do some table-pounding at the Foreign Office.

Seeing him, after more than two weeks of uncertainty and rising tension, did wonders for crew morale. There was a party that night that made up in spirit what it lacked in food and drink.

John went into town the next morning with Charles and stayed the next two nights, still haunting the building where the Foreign Secretary bicycled to work.

Mike, working in the yard at the hospital, looked up to see a DC-3 transport overhead, flying north. He wondered who would be flying DC-3s on the airlift, especially in the daytime.

Then he saw the markings: Federal Nigeria. It was one of the planes delivering reinforcement troops to the front between Aba and Umuahia. Fighting was now so close that the planes, he learned, were using the main road south of Umuahia as an airstrip and were taking off directly over Umuahia and Uzuakoli.

As they worked that morning, Mike and Tony talked about "old times"—the lives they had lived before Mercy Missions. It seemed incredible that all this had begun less than two months before. Why had they come? The time when the main pull to Biafra had been the excitement of a flying trip, or a chance to make a good movie, seemed a long way back.

The crew members had never really talked much about their motivation for coming. But now Mike admitted that he was getting involved in the troubles of the Biafrans. "Even if we get out," he told Tony, "I'd like to come back when our papers are cleared."

And Tony confessed that he felt much the same way. He wanted to go back to England just for one reason, he said: to put together a film that would wake up the people there to what was happening in Biafra. If they see what the crew had seen, he reasoned, they would come to feel the way the crew now did.

At 1 P.M. that day Norman Honey arrived from a trip to town with a message: "Get Ray's things together and take them to the hospital. It looks as though you're leaving."

Tony and Mike downed a quick lunch, borrowed a car, begged some gasoline and raced over the rutted roads into town.

The town seemed surprisingly quiet, but the Queen Elizabeth Hospital was more crowded than they had ever seen it.

Before seeing Ray they went to the manager of the hospital to see if Ray's release had been okayed. "Sorry, chaps," he said. "There's been a misunderstanding. There is no release for Ray or any of you, yet."

Discouraged, they wandered over to the Middelkoops' house. It was a gathering spot for Europeans, especially because there always was a cup of tea there.

Count Carl Gustav Von Rosen, the big blond Swedish airman, was there, and a packet of goodies had just arrived from Mrs. Middelkoop's relatives in Amsterdam.

The Count was a great story-teller, one of those personalities who dominates every room he's in. But today he seemed distracted, especially after he learned that the Mercy Missions crew still hadn't received either passes to move about or clearances to leave.

That afternoon they could hear the Nigerian bombs

dropping on the front to the north, and then see the twin-jet bombers circle right over Umuahia for another bombing run. They were low enough that the group at the Middelkoops could see the Nigerian markings on the wings.

John decided to stay in town to make another try in the morning. Before Mike and Tony started back for Uzuakoli, they said good-bye to Charles Bailiff and to Dave Duncan, another WCC representative, who were leaving that night. The number of Europeans being evacuated each night was growing steadily, as their organizations ordered them out for their own safety.

Saturday brought the news that the Uturu airstrip had fallen. This was hard to believe, simply because nobody wanted to. There had been no traffic for days in or out of Uli, which was surrounded on three sides by Federal troops within ten miles. If Uli were closed, there would be no way for them to leave Biafra.

Mike lay awake most of the night listening for a plane, even one, to go over Uzuakoli on the familiar west-to-east approach to Uli. It was the longest, loneliest night of his life. No planes came.

And it wasn't until late the next morning, Sunday, that he learned that Uli was still operating—that the planes going in and out of that strip were now using a different approach route.

Tony came over to Greg's house that morning, and he and Mike lazed around, listening to the radio and reading. Tony had been complaining for two days of a severe stomachache—"those bloody yams"—but refused Norman Honey's suggestion that he go to Queen Elizabeth Hospital to find out what was wrong. "If I go in there," he said, "I won't get out for six months. I don't want to be left here."

John returned from Umuahia and started packing;

he seemed confident that the okay to leave would come soon. And maybe for insurance, the crew joined Greg and a large congregation of Biafrans at church that night. The sermon was about world peace.

After church, Greg and Norman also started packing; they had been ordered by their superiors to get out now while they could. Both were miserable about having to leave the refugee camp with no one in charge. They also knew there was no chance of getting most of their personal belongings out. Mike and Tony agreed, if they were released, to take some of Greg's things along with them.

Everyone was up at dawn on Monday, September 23, for an early start into Umuahia. The car worked perfectly, for once, but when they got to the Middelkoops' house, there still was no word. John and the doctor left for the Foreign Office.

Mrs. Middelkoop, with a "Don't sit there doing nothing," gave Mike and Tony a big sack of egg powder and put them to work filling little bags with three spoonfuls each. When that was done, she put them to work sorting groceries and medicines in the hospital compound.

When John and Dr. Middelkoop came back, the others knew by their grins that the okay had finally come.

They went right to the hospital and told Ray the news. But he wouldn't believe it. "You're putting me on," he said, "and not a very funny joke either."

14

It used to happen occasionally that the beautiful administrative machine would break down and everybody would agree that it could not be repaired. For want of better, men would be substituted for the machine. And men would save France.

—Flight to Arras

JOHN and his crew didn't know at the time (and wouldn't know until months later, in fact) that Bailiff had resorted to a form of blackmail to get the Biafrans to turn them loose.

He had been firing cablegrams and making $65 phone calls to Church World Service in New York, where the Africa desk is manned by a huge, intense Dutchman named Jan Van Hoogstratten. (Actually, "desk" is not the way to describe the assignment of a man who rarely sits down. Van Hoogstratten, who had been working at top speed *before* the Nigeria-Biafra crisis, is usually seen striding from one office to another in New York's Interchurch Center or racing off to the airport to keep up with the task of getting emergency relief to half a dozen critical areas all over Africa.)

Bailiff, who had been with CWS less than six weeks, was demanding permission from Van Hoogstratten to tell the Biafrans that the whole church-supported airlift from São Tomé would come to a screeching halt unless the Mercy Missions crew was released at once.

This would affect four-fifths of all the relief food going in at that time. It might also affect the families—

some of them wives and children of top Biafran officials—who were being evacuated on return flights.

Bailiff was really getting worried, and not just because of the fact that the Federal troops were moving so fast toward complete victory (and their promised slaughter of the Mercy Missions crew).

Count Von Rosen, who still had the ear of the Biafran government, had told Charles: "If you don't get that crew out of here in another week, the Biafrans will surely hang them."

In New York, the cables and calls had set off long, agonizing discussions for the Church World Service Staff. What were the moral and ethical implications of a church agency resorting to such tactics? What would they do if the Biafrans called their bluff? Could they actually cut off food for half a million people because of concern over four lives? And were they putting a higher value on the lives of white Europeans than of black Africans?

There was a practical question too: Church World Service was only one partner, although a large one, in Norchurchaid. Would Caritas, the German and Scandinavian churches, and the World Council of Churches agree to such a move?

The discussions eventually involved relief officials in half a dozen countries, but they showed the ability of institutions to move fast when they have to. Within two days Charles Bailiff had his answer: permission granted.

When he had landed in Biafra, he had brought this message. And two days after he left, John Smith had been called to the State House and told, "You are to leave Biafra tonight."

15

Men travel side by side for years, each locked up in his own
silence or exchanging those words which carry no freight—till danger
comes. Then they stand shoulder to shoulder. They discover that
they belong to the same family. They wax and bloom in the
recognition of fellow-beings. They look at one another and smile.

—*Wind, Sand and Stars*

THEY carried Ray to the airplane in a brewery
van.

John had worked out a deal with the local brewery
to rent two vans, the only transport available, and
they started loading up at five o'clock in the afternoon.

George Orlick, the UNICEF public-relations man,
drove the van into which Ray was loaded; Mike sat
beside him to steady the cot. Tony drove the second
van, John followed in the temperamental Peugeot from
Uzuakoli, and a lorry full of spare parts brought up
the rear; it would return with food from the planes.

They had to go about sixty miles, across most of
what was left of Biafra, to Uli airstrip on the eastern
border. The roads were rough, unpaved and rarely
repaired.

The lorry driver was the one who knew the way to
Uli. But soon after sunset, before they had covered
fifteen miles, his headlights failed. The convoy stopped,
and after much poking and prodding, with plenty of
advice from all concerned, the driver announced he
was unable to get the lights to work again. The convoy
went on.

"We had to stop and ask directions at every cross-
roads," Mike recalls. "And of course, most of the local

people at one time or another had sworn not to say where it was. It was a big national secret."

There were several detours because some citizens, rather than refusing to talk, gave the convoy false directions.

Then, when they seemed to be getting within five miles of Uli, the clutch on Tony's van failed. Every time the convoy stopped, everyone would have to get out and push Tony, then rush to get in their own vehicles to catch up.

They arrived at the airstrip at nine o'clock and checked in at the dilapidated tin-roofed shack known officially as the State House. They arranged passage on a Balair chartered DC-6, and then tried to figure out how to get Ray, who still suffered pain from every jolt, into the cargo hold of the plane twelve or fifteen feet above the ground.

Eventually someone found a forklift. It wasn't working, of course, but they fiddled around with it until it was. Then they gently lifted Ray, high on morphine, into the waiting plane.

The night scene at Annabelle was a weird one, lit by the flicker of the makeshift gooseneck flares along the edge of the runway. These had to be faint enough not to guide bombers to the site, but bright enough to help a plane that had felt its way down to an altitude of forty or fifty feet. They were tin cans with what looked like an inverted funnel on top; a wick protruded from the tip of the funnel.

Their major drawback was that when one of the big Norchurchaid or Red Cross planes landed, its propellers would blow out the lights as it rolled down the runway, leaving a wake of darkness.

At intervals along the edge of the runway, and in several places around the State House, were trenches into which everyone could dive in case one of the Nigerian bombers attacked. Not long before, a rocket attack had killed eleven people at Uli, and everyone was still jumpy.

The control tower at Uli was on a truck hidden in the bush, ready to be driven out of reach if a bombing attack started. Sometimes there would be half a dozen planes circling overhead at the same time, without navigation lights, waiting for the radio call to come in and land.

Each plane had to be laden with enough fuel for the full round trip, because there wasn't any to spare at Uli.

And sometimes, as they circled overhead, the Connie pilots would see a Nigerian jet come in low and fast and drop bombs around the strip. If the bombs hit the runway, the airlift planes had to go on back without landing.

As soon as a plane had landed and rolled to a stop, a truck full of students would come roaring up; in the light of torches shielded from the sky, the students would unload the plane.

Within thirty minutes of landing time the plane would be off for São Tomé.

Each cargo was planned for a specific group of feeding centers and included exactly enough fuel for the trucks that would deliver it. Thirty-six hours after the food arrived a feeding station would be unloading it from a truck and repackaging it for distribution.

One of the supervisors at the airstrip explained the mathematics of the airlift to the men from Uzuakoli.

Every plane load of high-protein food assured minimal care—enough to keep malnutrition from getting any worse—for 1,000 people at a refugee camp for twenty days. Since the Norchurchaid airlift had started on August 17 (the day Mercy Missions had left

São Tomé for Fernando Po) it had made 175 flights. The number was growing; on one night the previous week there had been thirty round trips.

But the number of hungry people was growing too; the food was not enough to reach the people in the villages outside the feeding centers. The next step, the supervisor said, was to supplement the airlift food with locally-grown food from the northern part of Biafra. Some places in the north, he said, had a surplus crop but couldn't get it to areas where it was needed.

After Ray was safely aboard, John and Mike and Tony went back to the State House to complete the formalities. "There were so many people running around it was hard to find out who was in charge.

"And they were so trigger happy, every once in a while there would be a sudden burst of machine-gun fire."

Eventually they found the proper persons to stamp their papers—the stamps still read "Enugu"—and pronounce them ready to go. Right to the very end red tape dogged them. As the men settled back with a sigh and felt the DC-6 start down the runway toward freedom and home, each man was clutching two pieces of paper.

They were two mimeographed forms, one on lined tablet paper, which seemed to be the only thing the government had available. They were an Authorization to Ride in Red Cross Aircraft and a Biafran government Permission to Travel Abroad.

Epilogue

SEPTEMBER, 1968, was a low point in Biafra's fight to survive. Soon after the Mercy Missions crew left, France stepped up her flights of arms and ammunition into the besieged area. The Federal advance stalled, and for more than six months the lines held just about in the same place.

In March, 1969, Nigeria began another "final offensive." On Easter Sunday, Uzuakoli finally fell, its buildings shattered by two weeks of artillery and machine-gun fire.

Umuahia fell a week later, and the administrative headquarters of Biafra was moved to Orlu, sixty miles to the east. But the Biafrans bounced back, re-capturing Owerri, which had fallen in September.

The war ground on, mostly as a series of guerrilla encounters, and Lagos again stopped talking about a final offensive.

The troubles of the International Committee of the Red Cross continued, and were compounded by disagreements with the new government of Fernando Po —now called Equatorial Guinea—after it gained its independence from Spain. Eventually the ICRC had to move from the island, and began relief flights from

Cotonou, Dahomey. By March, 1969, the sum of all the ICRC flights into Biafra had reached 10,000 tons.

By the same date, the total of church-sponsored flights was 20,000 tons. The American Jewish Committee, representing twenty-two Jewish agencies, had joined Church World Service and Catholic Relief Services in sponsoring Jointchurchaid, a new international agency for relief flights. It included the old Norchurchaid, and in its first month, March, doubled the average tonnage to 5,000 a month.

The United States government had finally stopped playing games with the relief agencies, and sold eight giant C-97 Stratocruisers, at a nominal $3,600 apiece —four to Jointchurchaid and four to the ICRC.

The airlift was costing $100,000 a day, most of it coming from the USA, Canada and Europe. Dr. James MacCracken, director of Church World Service, called the effort "a miracle—indicating that Western man is no longer willing to tolerate mass starvation."

From September to March, according to the best available information, the number of Biafrans dying of starvation dropped from 6,000 a day to 200 a day.

The willingness of churches and synagogues to support this unprecedented effort still amazed those who raised the funds. But attempts at a long-range solution —an end to the fratricidal war—continued to involve only a few. England's Save Biafra Committee, which could raise $10,000 over a weekend for Mercy Missions, asked the same people for money to continue its lobbying against British involvement in the war—and received less than $250.

Tony Stancomb collapsed the day after he arrived in Fernando Po and underwent emergency surgery for—"from eating too many yams," he says.

Mike and Ray flew home in the cargo hold of an oil company plane on October 3.

John Smith stayed on in Fernando Po for more than a month, trying to clear the way for a new start for Mercy Missions. But the Biafrans were still suspicious. And with the airlift active again, there wasn't the pressure to get another set of flights going.

Peter Cadogan cabled that Nick's plane had been fixed, but that there was no money for gasoline to fly it to Fernando Po.

"We hadn't budgeted for accidents," Peter said later. "And we could hardly go back to our donors on the basis of Mercy Missions' accomplishments so far and ask them for another four thousand pounds."

Finally convinced that Mercy Missions was dead, at least as far as the Biafran emergency was concerned, John flew back to a cold England in November.

Six months later a visitor to Camberley would have found Mike Draper driving a truck, at three times the salary he had made in the bank.

"It doesn't have the security," he says, "but I don't worry so much about security now."

Ray Roberts, who still limps a little when he's tired, was back in Watford and busier than before as a free-lance photographer. "The editors know me now," he admits, "as that crazy photographer who'll do anything."

Tony had completed his film. It was too late to help Mercy Missions, but he was working to get it booked as a short subject in theaters to interest people in the needs of Biafra.

And John was without a job. Brushing back his shock of black hair and smiling, he said, "I've got the reputation for being an adventurer now, just because of this trip. And nobody wants to hire a pilot who's an adventurer."

There was a three-weeks-old baby girl in the house, along with Sue and Sennen-Dee. John was looking for any kind of job he could get.

"But if I had my choice," he said, "we'd still go back down to Fernando Po and fly supplies into Biafra."

The men were all apologetic about the "failure" of the mission. They felt that if the breaks had gone a little differently, or if the second plane had arrived, or if the Red Cross had been willing to give them the cargo and the codes, the ending of the story might have been much different.

And each man indicated that he thought the whole thing would be worth doing again.

Not just because it forced the Red Cross to begin its flights again at least a month before it had planned, at a time when 6,000 children were dying of hunger every day.

Not just because it helped break the silence of the British press on Biafra by providing a story that no amount of government disapproval could suppress.

They seemed to feel it would be worth doing again because of what it proved to each man about himself.

Ray Roberts, in a taped interview in Watford, talked about the decision to drop food at Uzuakoli:

We were anxious to do something. We were getting pretty desperate. We were also beginning to look slightly foolish.

And I suppose to some extent we wanted to set some kind of example. You don't go out on great crusading missions, with blazing humanitarianism on your sleeve, you know.

To some extent it was an adventure. As far as I

am concerned, it was an interesting journalistic situation. And at the same time, for a few weeks at least, it was an opportunity to lead a slightly less selfish life than I'd been leading up till then. It wasn't entirely journalistic, from my point of view at any rate.

I don't know what the others felt. I'm most suspicious—I have a special skepticism about humanitarians. Unless they're Albert Schweitzer, or Alfred Nobel, or Dag Hammarskjöld, or whoever.

I mean I judge them by their actions, and the amount of hardship they're willing to put up with, and the amount of effort they're willing to put into what they say they're going to do.

And I think that my colleagues turned out pretty well in that respect.

MERCY MISSIONS

Receipts and Payments Account
13th July to 9th November, 1968

RECEIPTS:

Donations £6,622.19.10.

PAYMENTS:

Cost of 2 Avro Anson air-craft	£3,500. 0. 0.	
Spare parts for aircraft	865.19. 1.	
Servicing of aircraft	195. 0. 0.	
Aircraft insurance	62. 4. 0.	
Pilots expenses, landing fees etc.	1,161.15. 9.	
Fuel for aircraft (paid to date)	207. 3. 5.	
Advance clearance cables for landing	106.19.10.	
Flight stationery, log books etc.	34.11. 0.	
Contribution towards 3rd Anson—Certificate of Airworthiness and Fuel Tank fitments (to be re-paid)	250. 0. 0.	
Administrative costs, ad-vertising etc.	130. 2.11.	
Secretary's expenses visit-ing Biafra	18.10. 8.	

Cash at Bank and in hand
at 11. 9.1968   6,532. 6. 8.   £ 90.13. 2.

I have checked this Receipts and Payments Account and certify that it is in accordance with the books and records of Mercy Missions.

N.J. HARDING, A.C.A.

13, Goodwin Street, London N.4.

Acknowledgments

In 15,000 miles of travel and many hours of interviews, I became indebted to many kind and helpful people. But the contributions of the following were more than helpful; they were essential to this book:

The men of Mercy Missions and their families; Charles Bailiff; Hannah Baneth and Peter Cadogan of the Save Biafra Committee; Hugh Samson, Rosemary Culley and Philip Watts of Noble and Samson Ltd.; Jan Van Hoogstratten, who casually handed me a newspaper clipping that started the whole thing; Nancy Nicalo, John Mullen and John Abbott for editorial help and background information; Dr. Leslie C. Sayre, director of the Committee on World Literacy and Christian Literature, for patience and understanding, and especially Mike Draper, who had the foresight to write things down while they were happening.

The quotations at the chapter headings are from books by Count Antoine de Saint-Exupéry, who as a pilot forty years ago pioneered the route along which Mercy Missions flew. They are from *Wind, Sand and Stars* (1939) and *Flight to Arras* (1942), copyrighted by William Heinemann Ltd.

B. H.